The Ten Best
Latin American Films
of the Decade
(2000–2009)

CINEMA TROPICAL PRESENTS

The Ten Best Latin American Films of the Decade (2000–2009)

Foreword and Editor: Carlos Gutiérrez

Jorge Pinto Books Inc.
New York

The Ten Best
Latin American Films
of the Decade
(2000–2009)

Associate editor: Richard Shpuntoff

Translators: Richard Shpuntoff and Pedro Ielpi

Cover design by Mara Behrens, www.maromadesign.com

Book design by Charles King, www.ckmm.com

ISBN10: 1-934978-39-6
ISBN13: 978-1-934978-39-9

Contents

Foreword

Latin American cinema has reinvented itself once again. The first decade of the new century has witnessed an unexpected and astonishing film renaissance throughout the region that has taken everybody by surprise. With no bells and whistles, no dogmas nor manifestos, and largely influenced and inspired by the experience of the so-called New Argentine Cinema, a young and enthusiastic generation of filmmakers have been drastically changing how Latin America sees and represents itself on the big screen. This trend, which has gone hand in hand with the major regional political shifts, along with the empowerment of local civil society, has produced an impressive body of artistic work and launched the professional careers of many filmmakers that through their work are challenging traditional notions of politics, culture and identity. And fortunately, this fertile trend hasn't shown signs of tiring yet.

This recent continental trend didn't materialize out of nowhere. Latin America has had a strong and outstanding film tradition—albeit full of ups and downs due to the variable sociopolitical and economic contexts of the region—and there had been comparable antecedents (at least to a certain degree). Latin America stormed the international scene once before in the 1960s and 1970s with the movement known as New Latin American Cinema, which was the first time that its cinema entered the international circuit as a substantial ground-breaking and highly-political faction, composed of different local movements such as the Brazilian Cinema Novo, the

Post-revolutionary Cuban Cinema and the Documentary Film School of Santa Fe (Argentina), among others. The filmmakers of the region played a preponderant and active role during this intense political and aesthetic movement helping theorize the movement under the banner of "Third Cinema" that helped create new models and paradigms of film production.

Yet due to numerous reasons, by the 80s the New Latin American Cinema movement had lost most of its original steam, and film production took a deep plunge for several years. It was in Argentina in the mid 90s, that filmmaker Martín Rejtman with his feature films *Rapado* unassumingly paved the road towards an independent mode of production, consciously breaking from the big themes and highly allegorical narratives of the preceding generation, to take a more minimalist and personal approach to filmmaking. Soon after, Bruno Stagnaro and Adrián Caetano's critically and popularly acclaimed *Pizza, birra, faso* officially heralded what would be christened as New Argentine Cinema—an amorphous yet committed group of young filmmakers in the process of challenging and rethinking traditional film narratives. It was Pablo Trapero's debut feature film *Mundo grúa* that would serve as the original emissary of this burgeoning trend to the international film circuit in 1999.

Shortly after, Mexico contributed with *Amores Perros*, Alejandro González Iñárritu's debut feature film and Grand Prize winner of the Critics Week the Cannes Film Festival, which is the film that opened the doors to Latin American cinema in the U.S., and its young and charismatic protagonist would provide an affable face to this new Latin American cinema trend. In a very short time, Mexican directors González Iñárritu, Alfonso

Cuarón and Guillermo del Toro (popularly known as the "Three Amigos"), along with their Brazilian counterparts Fernando Meirelles and Walter Salles, had built reputable internationally careers. Nonetheless they were only the very tip of the iceberg, as the region would end up fostering a very extensive generation of young filmmakers that ultimately is impelling the renovation in the cinema of the region.

What no one could ever foresee at the beginning of the new century was that this trend in Latin American cinema would be so long lasting and influential. It's been more than a decade now, and the generation of filmmakers has consolidated throughout the region, including those coming from countries that hadn't had a solid film tradition. Most of the filmmakers of this generation are in their thirties and forties, although younger filmmakers in their twenties are now joining the ranks, and most of them working with very modest budgets. Moreover, some seasoned directors from previous generations have remained active, in many cases still doing interesting work and in varying ways contributing their experience to the local cinemas. Countries like Uruguay, Colombia, Bolivia, and Chile, have greatly contributed to the revitalization of the cinema of the region, which has proved to be highly contagious. Take for instance Nicaragua—a country that hadn't produced a feature film in over 20 years, passed a comprehensive film law that hopefully will consolidate the nascent local scene.

One of the key characteristics of this trend resides in its diversity: of its modes of production, of its narratives, and of its artistic influences and intentions. Paradoxically, the lack of unifying aesthetics and narrative is perhaps the main reason that it hasn't been characterized as a film movement thus hindering its recognition. Regrettably, despite this great and amazing revitalization, the artistic output in Latin American cinema remains underrated and, in general, not validated by the international film community. For what these ten years have been for Latin American cinema, there's still very little critical and academic information, and most of the filmmaker's remain largely unknown—even within the international film circuit. It will be an enormous undertaking and revisionist process to fully understand this creative output and its implications, particularly trying to grasp Latin American cinema in its complexity, and beyond the traditional, outdated and limited notions of national cinema.

The creation of Cinema Tropical, perfectly coincided with the resurgence of Latin American cinema. The very first event that the organization held was a sold-out screening of Rejtman's *Silvia Prieto* with the filmmaker in attendance at the (now extinct) Pioneer Theater in New York City's East Village on February 19, 2001. The event that followed was a special sneak preview of the Mexican film *Amores Perros* attended by the then unknown director and protagonist. The organization got its start as a cine club organizing film series with weekly screenings at the Pioneer Theater, and soon expanded to create a non-theatrical circuit that would also hold regular screenings in thirteen of the most important *cinematheques* around North America including Facets Cinémathèque in Chicago, the NW Film Center in Portland, and the Museum of Fine Arts in Boston.

It was in 2003, that Cinema Tropical launched Caetano's film *Bolivia* as its first theatrical release at Film Forum in New York City, and to date the organization has done sixteen releases, more than any other film distributor in the country. Totally empirically and encouraged by this ebullient film production, the organization created different programming and promotional platforms with the aim of promoting the work of the filmmakers of the region. Today through a diversity of programs and initiatives, Cinema Tropical is thriving as a dynamic and groundbreaking media arts organization experimenting in creating better and more effective platforms for the distribution and exhibition of foreign cinema in this country, introducing American audiences to the rich and diverse tradition of Latin American cinema, as well as advocating inside and outside the film community for a more inclusive take on world cinema.

Under the suggestion and compilation of our colleague, filmmaker and blogger Mario Díaz, at the end of 2009 Cinema Tropical culled a poll amongst 32 New York-based film professionals—including critics, bloggers, festival programmers, distributors, and academics that have been active in promoting and disseminating Latin American film in the U.S. The participants were simply asked to provide their favorite top-ten list of Latin American films (those produced in a Latin American country and helmed by a Latin American director) released either commercially or via film festivals between 2000–2009. The survey itself was created with the goal of increasing awareness of Latin American film among the U.S. movie-going public and the film community as a whole.

We are totally aware of the limitations and injustices of such polls, yet it proved to be a very healthy and exciting exercise as the films got published throughout the Americas fostering a lively debate on Latin American cinema. The list has provided a particular taste of the diversity of the cinema of the region, as well-known international hits such as Meirelles's *City of God* and Cuarón's *Y Tu Mamá También* were paired with more intimate films such as Pablo Rebella and Juan Pablo Stoll's *Whisky* and Carlos Reygadas's arthouse favorite *Silent Light*. We were also glad that at least one documentary film *Bus 174* by José Padilha, co-directed with Felipe Lacerda, was included in the selection, as the region has proven to be equally prolific in the production of documentary films and hybrid forms, as it has in the production of fictions.

Probably the most surprising result of the poll was the fact that the three films made by Argentine director Lucrecia Martel made it to the Top Ten—her debut feature *La Ciénaga* landing in the number one spot. Not an easy achievement: it is highly uncommon that a young filmmaker can build such a vigorous and tour-de-force professional career maintaining the same level of rigor in three consecutive films. Undeniably, Lucrecia Martel has played a crucial role in the cinema of the region.

Based on the proposal and with the enthusiastic support of Jorge Pinto and his publishing house, we decided to create this book as a way to celebrate this decade of great Latin American cinema, with the aim of trying to reach a wider audience, as well as to offer some critical content that can help the international audience enjoy and contextualize the films better. We invited a diverse group composed of ten film critics and scholars to write a brief essay on each of the films selected in the top ten list, to create a polyphony of voices to continue and expand the debate on the works and the filmmakers. The selected contributors are not only from different nations (Argentina, Brazil, Chile, Mexico, U.K. and U.S.) and countries of residence, but also from different theoretical perspectives. Of course, this is not a definitive compilation, nor does it offer the final word on the films selected, but it is an attempt to contribute to the exciting diversity of Latin American cinema with an equally exciting diverse approach in the selection of contributors.

The publishing of this book is part of a larger and more ambitious project of Cinema Tropical celebrating recent Latin American cinema, a project that involves the launching of the Cinema Tropical Awards as well as a film series at the prestigious IFC Center in New York City. We offer this book for your consideration in the spirit of the truly exciting cinematic works that have been created by a new generation of Latin American filmmakers, in the hope that the next ten years prove to be at least as exciting and stimulating as these last ten have been, and with our desire that through this modest celebration we may contribute to the continuing promotion of the films and the filmmakers, and to their vital discussion.

—Carlos A. Gutiérrez

La Ciénaga (2001)
Images courtesy of Cinema Tropical

#1 .

Shipwreck in the Middle of the Mountain:

La Ciénaga

(Argentina, 2001)

I

The elements that make up *La Ciénaga* are very simple: an extremely hot summer, a country estate in the hinterlands of the province of Salta, and two families. Mecha, the owner of the house, has a small accident and her friend, Tali, visits her. Over the course of these days, the very different families of both women reunite and intermingle, the children coming and going, and a certain energy invades this otherwise withered summer home. José, Mecha's eldest son, travels from Buenos Aires to see his mother, the boys go hunting in the mountain, and the girls take their *siestas* together and chat at the edge of a pool full of stagnant, dirty water. Meanwhile, the women plan a trip to Bolivia to buy school supplies, but the trip never happens. Someone claims to have seen the Virgin and at the end of the film there is a tragic death. Not much else happens in this world as it is closely observed by Momi, the youngest of Mecha's daughters.

Lucrecia Martel said, "When one is a child, perhaps one does not understand many things, but one is much more perceptive. This was a key to the camera placement: to not try and be descriptive, because I didn't trust that showing things would clarify anything." It suggests an intense and extremely sensitive perception, even when it is a partial or insufficient perception for decoding what is going on: the camera framing takes in the actions from an eccentric position and her decision to highlight or mute certain elements in a scene produces a slightly odd tone.

II

The film regularly takes detours as it moves forward, avoiding something unmentionable that we cannot see, but that constantly threatens to make itself present. This uncertainty, that haunts the image, is embedded there from the very beginning by means of a strictly audiovisual modulation.

We never really know what are the dimensions of *La Mandrágora* (Mecha's property), its property lines, how far it is from the city of La Ciénaga, where Tali lives. Nor are we shown the spatial relationships of the house that would allow us to reconstruct its layout. It is impossible to figure out how many bedrooms there are or where they are in relation to each other. Like in a prison or an island suspended in the middle of limbo, the summer home of Mecha and her family appears to be separated from everything and offers no possibility of escape. The spaces are not connected within a continuum; it is better to say that they are assaulted by "interruptions," as if a space were invading or raping the next space. There is no traveling, no transitions, no displacements. We never see a character go from one place to another. When we realize someone has arrived in a place it is because she or he is already there. And so the metaphor of the title is clear, because this is exactly what a swamp is: we are aware of its existence when it is too late and we have begun to sink into the mud.

This same kind of manipulation is evident in the way Martel works with time. All of the action in the film takes place in a few days, from Mecha's accident to Luciano's death. Nonetheless, the lack of events, the rituals that are repeated over and again, the weary movements of the characters and the general inaction (nobody has anything to do: everybody is just killing time waiting for summer to end) lends an impression that things are happening in slow motion or, even, in a state of suspension. The film takes place during the days of Carnival but, significantly, this is a minor anecdote: the forces of regeneration and transformation that belong to the *life cycles* associated with Carnival are like a backdrop against which we see the *vicious cycles* of the characters, far from any possibility of change. So in the same way that we cannot see any spatial boundaries, we cannot notice any teleology in the passing of time. The time of *La Ciénaga* is a thickened one that drags the characters down to a static bottom that prevents them from taking action. The metaphor here is the *siesta*: eternity suspended in these summer afternoon naps, populated by terrible and legendary stories.

The space-time framework, therefore, does not depend upon the mere recording, but rather on a subtle but elaborated chronotope within the film's interior. The image does not so much inform about a time and place as it uses time and place for the purpose of expression.

III

This system of dramatic coordinates established by this swampy space and arrested time defines a certain kind of treatment of plot. How does one create a narrative progression made of dramatic plateaus? In what way should one organize the conflicts in the absence of a story? Martel explains that, when the script for *La Ciénaga* was awarded at the Sundance Festival, she was advised to change her original plan and select only one or two of the main characters and organize the entire narration around them. The filmmaker's resistance consisted in maintaining an apparently undefined structure that dispensed with the narrative skeleton that is provided by a conventional plot.

Often, the shot does not begin where something is happening but rather it discovers or seems to run into an event already in progress. The camera manages to see it but, at the same time, gives the feeling that it could have just as well missed it. As if it did not control the situation, the camera enters into a flow that is exterior and prior to it, without really knowing what it must capture from the situation. The editing, on the other hand, functions in the opposite way: it intentionally stays on the frame when it should have cut or it cuts before the action is over. In one way or another, there is an excess of down time or a lack of closure and, as such, virtually, the situations are continually generating consequences. They continually resound, like an echo, over the following scenes.

The camera does not know what to see or how, while the editing imposes when to see and for how long. Just like the characters of the film, the viewer is caught between these two fires: anything can happen and it is impossible to foresee how things will develop. "Each person sees what they're able to," says Tali about the appearance of the Virgin. It is impossible to anticipate when, where and how she will appear. Just like the faithful pilgrims going to the makeshift altar, the gaze of the spectator does not control what he or she sees, but rather is at the mercy of the events that—like the Virgin—appear suddenly in the most unexpected place. That is why the ellipsis and what is outside of the camera frame matter as much as what appears within the frame. That which the framing or the editing excludes puts dramatic pressure upon that which is shown.

Momi dives in and does not return to the surface. The shot stays on this muddy mirror of water that remains still and, since the shot is excessively long, the quietude ends up becoming disturbing. In the following scene, a bit later, the kids chat nonchalantly around the pool. Momi does not seem to be among them. In truth, she is just out of the framing of the shot and, when the shot finally shows her, it does so as if nothing had happened. The film is not aware of the effect of the danger that it obligates us to take heed of. The line that separates one thing from another is thin and capricious. Like Russian roulette: nothing happened, although it could have been a tragedy. And at some moment it will end up being one. While the boys hunt in the mountain, Luciano remains in the line of fire; someone warns him to go away and, although the cut leaves the action off screen, we hear in the distance the shot of a rifle. Minutes later, nevertheless, Luciano reappears nonchalantly around the scene, as if the film again takes away the importance of this extremely dramatic moment.

The off camera gunshot and the suppression of what follows is not a question of narrative economy but rather a dramatic modulation: Martel is not omitting a "dead time" in the film (since the event has a central importance) but rather she is turning the situation into a bomb about to explode. What is eliminated returns enhanced like a terrible memory in the contiguous images, a contained violence, an invisible mark that nevertheless leaves its imprint on the other shots. First, the concern is "they're going to kill him," then it will be "they could have killed him." But always, what happens is more than what happens: this continuous piling on of threats. The entire film stakes itself on a dialectic between rest and movement: the calm of what we see and the imperceptible flow of what is rearing up from below. The succession of small accidents and risky situations never modifies the characters' behaviors. This produces a conflictive accumulation and, as a consequence, a growth of dramatic tension that can only be resolved by a catastrophe. There is no logical curve that, through a game of cause and effect, will lead to an outcome; rather there is an expansion of material that is just about to explode.

IV

Each shot (and each sequence of shots) functions like a receptacle in which it seems nothing happens. And although this imposes a free-floating, distracted or inactive attention, in a gradual or invisible way something violent is incubating that later, when it emerges, will be surprising. The death of Luciano is a catastrophe: because of its tragic dimensions and because of its apparent unpredictability.

Suddenly there is a change of speed, an acceleration. At first sight, this resolution might seem untimely and cruel, but it isn't. And there are two reasons for this. On one hand, the death has been anticipated in details throughout the film: at the beginning, Luciano is intrigued by the dead rabbit on the marble of the kitchen, he hurts his leg and it is clear that this is a reoccurring situation (Tali says to Rafael, "he got cut again"), later he tries holding his breath and stops breathing, on one of the expeditions to the mountain he places himself between the rifle and the target, during a game the girls chase him and they force him to play dead. On the other hand, the accident would be a low blow if not for the Martel's filming it from a distance, as if she prefers not to see it. We understand that it was foreseeable and unforeseeable at the same time. The camera does not emphasize the episode. It shows it for what it is: an absurd event that becomes a tragedy.

Martel's intelligence consists in delaying the outcome and in making this deferment occur without warning so that it explodes unexpectedly. When Tali has to put the trip to Bolivia on hold, she is able to convince herself of the risks that it holds for them and reasons that, in the end, it is for the best: "so we can avoid a disaster." Curiously, the accident occurs a bit later. Perhaps if they had taken the trip, Luciano would not have fallen from the ladder. Or perhaps he would have died a week later. Or it would have happened to someone else. The connecting of events is a matter of chance and, as such, uncontrollable. Everyone is free to their (good or bad) luck.

Luciano dies because he does and the only thing this reveals is a great emptiness. In this sense, the trajectory of the child (abandoned to whatever could happen to him) is set up against that of Momi (the only one that, in the end, painfully, has learned something) although they have complementary effects: he dies without seeing anything and she discovers that there is nothing to see.

From the beginning, the path of Luciano towards death does nothing more than confirm itself, in a veiled but progressive manner; Momi, on the other hand, begins thanking heaven for letting her be near Isabel and, in the end, discovers that there is nothing to see in that place where the Virgin is supposed to be waiting to fulfill the prayers of the faithful. This game of knowing and not knowing defines the tone of the film. Although they are very different ages, Momi and Luciano are the most innocent and credulous of each family. But while the fantasies of Luciano never stop growing throughout the film, Momi passes from devotion to clarity.

Other than her, nobody realizes that it is necessary to become aware and take responsibility. For good or for bad, nothing can be done because any possibility of change depends upon a greater will beyond that of the characters. Or people die because of fate or they stake their salvation on the miracles of the Virgin. But in either case, the possibility of constructing some meaning to existence seems to be out of reach for each one of the characters. Distilled by comfort, custom or stagnation, the explanations come out paradoxically tranquilizing. As if in some other place (never there, where the characters live) there exists a life that is more intense or more real.

V

In one scene, we see a cow that has fallen into the swamp: the boys that are playing in the mountain know that once it has begun to sink there is no way to save it and that the only merciful thing to do is shoot it. Just like the cow, everyone in Mecha's family and in Tali's sink inevitably. Things tend to become stagnant. According to legend, one day Mecha's mother got in her bed and never again left her bedroom. This ghost weighs upon the woman like a family mandate: very few times do we see her get up and almost never without her nightgown.

Mecha has inherited a rural business built around the cultivation and sale of regional products. The peppers that we see on a tray at the beginning of the film are the basis of a family business that is no longer profitable; but everyone is too numb to try and resuscitate it. It is possible to infer that in other times the business was more prosperous and that now it is headed towards bankruptcy. Nevertheless, the characters prefer to live as if the good times had not gone away and would last forever: as such, they don't notice that the water in the pool is dirty and that the house is falling apart. They don't understand that the rules of the market have changed. It is not surprising then that in this unproductive world (in which nothing changes and everything repeats itself, wearing out until nothing is left) things happen with the cruel logic of the inexorable within a circular structure. The beginning and the end, tragically identical, is the only thing that insinuates a structure within this series of events that are experienced by the characters without asking too much about why they behave as they do.

Perhaps, then, it isn't that strange that the narrative economy of the film exploits abandonment and the elements as much so as the closure and suffocation. These terms do not function as opposites but rather within a singular logic: the sensation of being enclosed is derived from the expanse. *La Ciénaga* exposes a state of things configured in such a way that any change seems far from the horizon of possibilities of the characters. The key consists in questioning one's self because none of them react, because none is aware that they are sinking without recourse. What Martel tries to understand (and make others understand) is that the absence of alternatives is not fatality but rather that the relationships between people have been dragged through a long process of social deterioration. In an askew way, we can see in the film what remains of Argentina after the military dictatorship of the 70s and the socioeconomic setbacks of the 80s and 90s.

How do we make a committed cinema? Martel says that her responsibility is to "maintain a critical vision of my situation as a woman of the Argentine middle class. This is the place in which I locate myself within the Argentine cinema. I think that in these terms the cinema has a political function." In an exemplary manner, *La Ciénaga* makes evident certain traditional roles and certain social attitudes that have been internalized by a middle class in decadence, as if it were a matter of fate or nature. In the film, there is a visual hermeneutic that bears witness in images to a certain state of things and, with the same movement, makes its critique. This intervention is a political one, and not because it sustains a particular ideology, but rather because it establishes a new community of the visible.

—David Oubiña

This text has been extracted from David Oubiña's *Estudio crítico sobre* La ciénaga, *de Lucrecia Martel*, Buenos Aires, Editorial Pic Nic, 2006.

#2

Amores Perros

(Mexico, 2000)

Ten years after the release of *Amores Perros* marks a fine point to look back at what made this feature so ground-breaking and what ensures its continuing importance today. This process requires a reconsideration of multiple aspects of the film: its production process and scripting, its depiction of gender and the city, and its innovative technique in both sound and vision.

To begin with, the production process. *Amores Perros* was, of course, the first feature by then unknown director Alejandro González Iñárritu who had a background in the populist media of radio deejay-ing and TV advertising. Whereas Mexican cinema had long been dependent on state support with its attendant dangers of cronyism and political control, *Amores Perros* was funded by private companies—González Iñárritu's Zeta and, majority stakeholder, Altavista—a truly unusual move at the time. Proud of their independence, *Amores Perros*'s executive producers, Francisco González Compeán and Marta Sosa, saw their film as parallel to the momentous shift in Mexican politics which coincided with its release: the loss of power of the PRI government which had ruled the country for some seventy years.

It was no accident, then, that after its enormous local and international success, *Amores Perros* should receive a special outdoor screening in Mexico City's central square, the Zócalo, the symbolic centre of the nation. Moreover, Altavista's modest, but canny, ambition was to make low budget, quality features that could truly connect with local audiences and thus pay their way in the domestic market. *Amores Perros* was also helped by a rare publicity blitz that rivaled Hollywood in its professionalism: the hugely stylish, and oddly shaped, press books given out in Cannes, where the film triumphed in the Critics' Week section, remain collectors' pieces.

A decade later González Iñárritu is an established transnational auteur: *21 Grams* (2003) was shot in Memphis, *Babel* (2006) took him as far as Morocco and Japan, and *Biutiful* (as yet unreleased theatrically) is set in Barcelona. González Iñárritu has thus established with two other nomadic directors, Guillermo del Toro and Alfonso Cuarón a new form of filmmaking that uniquely triangulates Mexico, the U.S., and Europe. And if Altavista has been eclipsed by its globetrotting protégé, the template of the local blockbuster remains: their glossy

Amores Perros (2000)
Image courtesy of Lionsgate Entertainment

historical epic *Arráncame la vida* (*Tear This Heart Out*), little seen abroad, was the domestic success story of 2008.

Central to *Amores Perros*'s original success was its innovative plotting by screenwriter Guillermo Arriaga, from whom González Iñárritu is now artistically separated. As is well known, the film tells three separate stories, linked by the traumatic event of a car crash, which is depicted three times from different perspectives. Poor Octavio (a disconcertingly youthful Gael García Bernal) gets involved with dog fighting in order to win money to elope with his sister-in-law Susana (the moving Vanessa Bauche), media executive Daniel (Álvaro Guerrero) leaves his wife for Spanish supermodel Valeria (Goya Toledo), and terrorist turned hit man El Chivo (Emilio Echevarría) signs on to a kidnapping involving rival businessmen brothers Luis and Ramiro (Jorge Salinas, Marco Pérez). Fitting together the fragments of this complex narration proved testing. The final cut differs considerably from the shooting script and González Iñárritu benefited greatly from the input of del Toro, who reportedly slept on his couch at a crucial stage in the edit. Yet *Amores Perros* feels all of a piece, its multiple plot strands organically linked by surface similarities (all of the characters own dogs of different breeds) and deep-level continuities (all of them engage in infidelity, implicitly contrasted with the faithfulness of their canine companions).

Thanks to *Amores Perros*'s brilliantly innovative structure, ten years later multi-plot narratives feel over-familiar, from the Oscar-winning platitudes of *Crash* (Paul Haggis, 2004) to González Iñárritu's subsequent, and arguably less accomplished, features. By the time Arriaga came to direct his own feature (*The Burning Plain*, 2008), the format was exhausted; and, marking a radical shift, *Biutiful* is, it would appear, a character study of a single tragic individual. But, aside from its plotting, *Amores Perros*'s treatment of women, perhaps its most controversial aspect, already felt retrograde and stereotypical to some viewers at the time. Maternal and vulnerable, Susana is a Madonna, trapped with her child in a home that offers no support. Conversely, career woman Valeria is, if not a whore, at the very least vain and superficial, seducing her mature lover away from his wife and kids and apparently punished for her sexual activity.

With hindsight, however, gender relations in the film prove to be more problematic. When Octavio's plans come to naught and his brother is killed, Susana boldly chooses life alone rather than with the lover who has let her down so badly. When Valeria's looks are lost (her leg amputated after the accident), she faces with some maturity an uncertain future with a partner who has proved more supportive than one might have guessed. González Iñárritu's pervasive pessimism is here put on hold, perhaps, for a moment. And while Gael García's subsequent career was meteoric, embracing such critical and commercial successes as *Y Tu Mamá También* (2001) and *Bad Education* and *The Motorcycle Diaries* (both 2004), Vanessa Bauche's professional profile is less showy but highly dignified. Articulate and outspoken, she directed a documentary on the notorious unsolved murders of young women in Ciudad Juárez (*Femicidio, Hecho en México*, 2003).

Central to *Amores Perros*'s initial appeal was its image as a *chilango* feature, a film that embodied the unique pleasures and horrors of the megalopolis of Mexico City. But it is important to stress here that, contradicting First World clichés of "poor cinema," González Iñárritu paid as much attention to the capital's huge middle class as to its yet larger multitudes of working poor. Shot wholly on location, the feature gives us access to the cramped quarters of Octavio and Susana, crowded with kitsch ornaments, but also to the dream home of Daniel and Valeria, a coolly minimalist apartment. Businessmen pursue adulterous affairs in chic restaurants, while the hit men who pursue them live, like El Chivo, in spectacular squalor.

It is something of a shock to return (as I did recently) to the street corner in the trendy *colonia* of Condesa, where the cacophonous car crash was so brilliantly staged, and to find it calm and quiet, frequented in real life more by innocuous joggers than careering gunmen. And as if to prove that *Amores Perros*'s sense of the city was founded not on some intrinsic sense of place but on expert cinematic technique, cinematographer Rodrigo Prieto, whose career received a well deserved boost from the film, took his edgy and grainy look as far as Detroit for Curtis Hanson's surprisingly accomplished Eminem film, *8 Mile* (2002).

Amores Perros's pervasive influence, then, has been as much at the technical level of sound and vision as in the narrative realm of scripting and plotting. González Iñárritu demanded of Prieto a whole repertoire of techniques throughout the film's lengthy running time: in the first episode the shooting style is up close and hand held, matching the visceral excitement of the dog fights; in the second, it is calm and collected, with tripod shots mirroring the enforced stasis of the immobilized model; and in the third, it is sleek and fluid, with tracking and traveling shots that follow the hit man as he stalks his quarry.

Less self-evident, but yet more effective, is the subtle sound design. Barking dogs often accompany the action, way down in the mix; snatches of catchy songs come and go as characters drive the streets, heedless of the future shocks that await them. Keeping his arms in reserve, González Iñárritu waits almost an hour into the running time before employing Gustavo Santaolalla's haunting score with its carefully distinguished leitmotifs: Octavio's simple acoustic love theme contrasts with the synthesizer motif and rock steady drumming of the final episode.

Santaolalla, whose global career was launched by the film, was another vital contributor to *Amores Perros*. Proving as versatile as his colleague Prieto, both were to collaborate on *Brokeback Mountain* (Ang Lee, 2005), a film whose heartfelt ruralism could hardly be further from *Amores Perros*'s urgent and bloody urbanism. And, canny as ever, González Iñárritu had marketed *Amores Perros* to Mexico's youth audience (previously indifferent to local movies) by cross-promoting his feature with songs by major Mexican artists such as Julieta Venegas and Café Tacuba, which although not featured in the film were said to be inspired by it.

Finally, then, what has been the significance and influence of *Amores Perros*? It is difficult to remember now that, before the millennium, Mexican cinema (distant indeed from its massively popular Golden Age of the 1940s) had turned its back on its audience. More mature *auteurs* favored political films that held little interest for the youth who now thronged the new multiplexes. Although *Amores Perros* coincided fortuitously with a radical change in Mexico's form of government, it was clear that González Iñárritu's concerns were more moral and metaphysical than social and political. His great achievement, along with that of his friends and colleagues del Toro and Cuarón, is to have founded a third way of filmmaking that is carefully balanced between the purely commercial genres of Mexico's comedies and youth pictures, and hard-core art movies, as represented by the remarkable emergence over this decade of Carlos Reygadas and his followers. Although such features may have sociopolitical implications (del Toro's *Pan's Labyrinth* is one of the most sophisticated accounts of the legacy of the Spanish Civil War), this is not their primary focus. Indeed González Iñárritu's subsequent career has proved his belief that, to cite the title of a classic *telenovela*, "the rich also weep." Newly transnational in its ambitions and distribution, the Mexican prestige picture, of which *Amores Perros* is the first and outstanding example, is an enduring and wholly unexpected contribution to world cinema.

—Paul Julian Smith

Luz Silenciosa / Stellet Licht (2007)
Image courtesy of Palisades Tartan

#3

Silent Light

(Mexico, 2007):

Carlos Reygadas's Meditation

on Love and Ritual

"Peace is stronger than love."

Carlos Reygadas's third and most accomplished movie, *Stellet Licht* or *Silent Light* (2007), is a poetic meditation on life, love, ritual and spirituality. Set in present times in a Chihuahuan Mennonite community—Anabaptist Christians of Swiss and German descent—and spoken almost entirely in the medieval German dialect Plautdietsch, the movie is a first in the history of world cinema. Johan (Cornelio Wall Ferhr), a respected and decent farmer, father of six young children, married to Esther (Miriam Toews), finds himself involved in a love triangle with Marianne (Maria Pankratz). The affair is no secret to anyone, and Esther suffers in silence while Johan, the son of a preacher, tries to understand the true source of his love for Marianne: God or Satan. He believes that Marianne is his "natural woman" or the one that God chose for him, but at the same time knows he must be faithful to Esther. Johan turns to his father for advice but his father's only answer is that the decision must be Johan's and that he needs to make it before he loses both women. But then, suddenly, the heartbroken Esther dies.

In reaction, Marianne appears at Esther's wake, renounces love and, shattering all realism and narrative logic, gives Esther a tearful resurrection kiss that miraculously brings her back to life.

In his former films, Reygadas uses an almost defiantly realistic style to narrate simple stories. His feature length film debut, *Japón* (2002), follows Pedro (Alejandro Ferretis), a middle-aged man who claims to be a painter, as he travels to a remote corner of the sierra Tarahumara to commit suicide. At a tiny mountain hamlet he stays at the house of Asención (Magdalena Flores), an octogenarian woman, and ends up having sex with her. Engaging and intense, the film's minimal style, long silences and enthralling rhythm create a powerful sense of anguish and unpredictability. The explicit sex act is provocative and unusual and could be perceived as a cruel joke, a sadistic spectacle in which an elderly lady agrees to expose herself by having sex on-screen with the non-professional protagonist. In Reygadas's treatment, the act instead confronts the viewer with its striking humility and sincerity. The honesty of the flesh offers a revelation to which we cannot remain unmoved. This dose of *verité* is a shock treatment for the senses that works much like Bertold Brecht's *Verfremdungseffekt* ("distancing effect"), preventing the spectator from passively accepting a fictive narrative and forcing him or her out of his or her comfort zone into a territory where certitudes are questioned. Reygadas uses this technique in all his films.

We never really know why Pedro wants to kill himself or why he chooses a sacrifice in nature. What we have is Pedro's rediscovery of life through the shock of *dépaysement* and the sexual transgression into the realm of old age. Probably those are the reasons for the choice of the exotic title, which could also be interpreted as an allusion to the samurai culture and its dogma of suicide to escape defeat, humiliation or pain. But for Reygadas interpretation is absurd. Just as the reasons that took Pedro to the mountains are irrelevant, his personal history has no meaning. What matters is his redemption.

Japón captured the attention of the festival circuit and Reygadas was turned instantly into one of the most promising Mexican film directors of the 21st century. His second feature, *Battle in Heaven*, shown in competition at Cannes in 2005, is a strange hybrid: a rabidly funny commentary on modern day Mexico City, a society dominated by corruption, insecurity and chaos, as well as a painful reflection on guilt, love and death. In it a chauffeur named Marcos (Marcos Hernández) is infatuated with the woman he works for, Ana (Anapola Mushkadiz), the daughter of a wealthy politician. To supplement his income Marcos and his wife sell clocks at an informal stand in a subway station, but they've also decided to kidnap a neighbor's baby for the ransom. At the beginning of the movie Marcos finds out that the baby accidentally died while in his wife's care. Guilt makes him confess to Ana—who works at a high-end brothel called The Boutique, apparently for kicks. He accepts her suggestion to turn himself into the police, but comes to believe he needs a different kind of atonement and joins other penitents in a pilgrimage to the Basilica of Guadalupe.

Reygadas offers a plot that could be mistaken for a thriller, but only presents the perspective of a confused and extremely hurt Marcos, so the movie becomes a description of his struggle with reality, his efforts to ask for forgiveness and cleanse his consciousness. Tragedy intensifies his obsession with Ana, a woman he has known since childhood. The director doesn't need to explain Marcos's torment at seeing the object of his love and desire transform into a prostitute. As Reygadas put it in an interview in *Senses of Cinema*: "the spectator is Marcos." Here again, the explicit sex act scenes add an element of controversy and moral indignation. But rather than exploitation, the fact that the characters have sex is part of Reygadas's commitment to realism and he uses it to show how not even the closeness of body contact with Ana can remedy Marcos's tragic loneliness.

In *Stellet Licht*, which was awarded the Jury Prize at Cannes, Reygadas does not try to make an anthropological or ethnographical film. He presents the Mennonite people respectfully but with a certain distance. They represent a simple, egalitarian and modest society, with a hierarchical structure but no social classes, limited outside influence and almost no mass media. There is the radio but the only screen we see is a small TV in a van, in which Marianne, Johan and his kids watch a very sweaty and grimacing Jacques Brel singing *Les Bonbons* in concert in the 60s. Their world is familiar and at the same time alien; they use mechanical technology like cars, tractors and clocks (a constant and iconic reference to the mortality of men) but they could easily be transplanted two hundred years in the past without significant changes.

Stellet Licht is not a Mennonite movie but a film about people who still practice rituals, and whose domestic life is still dominated by ceremonial acts and the rhythms of nature. The director found in the simplicity of this community a perfect setting for archetypes and an absence of "distractions," much like the setting of a fairy tale. The film starts with a slow dawn which takes us from a primeval darkness to a series of bucolic scenes orchestrated with insects and farm sounds, and ends with an equally slow dusk in which the screen fades slowly into darkness and silence. Light creates all material things and its absence wipes them away. This way Johan's story is linked with the cosmos; his human drama occupies the center of creation, where the mundane and the sacred are intertwined. But these metaphors for the Genesis and the Apocalypse occur in the same physical space, the sunrise and sunset are filmed as happening on the same side of the sky, which could be seen as a mystery, as another miracle. The night is not really falling but the day is running backwards to repeat itself over and over again.

Every Reygadas film involves fervent religiosity, guilt and redemption. He dissects religion in order to separate it from spirituality, to isolate dogma and reconsider the true meaning of rituals. His work is about the sublime and the rhapsodic, the ecstatic and rapturous, life-changing emotions that cannot be reduced to words. His films, as with all great cinema, deal with characters in internal struggle, incapable of controlling their emotions. Pedro, Marcos and Johan each pursue his own personal method of escape: committing suicide, surrendering to the police, abandoning a wife. In *Stellet Licht* the sublime is everywhere and miracles are possible just as night turns into day. The natural elements seem to be in synchronicity with human emotions and every gesture carries transcendence: bathing a child in a pond or making love to a mistress could be fleeting encounters with divinity. Even the seasons seem to be nothing but a reflection of human joy, uncertainty or despair.

Reygadas puts his actors, most of them nonprofessionals, in uncomfortable situations. He pushes them to extremes of vulnerability, where they literally bare their bodies and feelings, where nakedness "can give access to internal knowledge," as Reygadas told *The Guardian* in 2005. His third feature film is cast almost entirely with Mennonites from that region with several recruited from Canada and Germany. The simple idea to put people from this extremely religious, insular and closed community not only on screen but also performing in the story of an adulterous relationship is surprising. The most basic transgression of this film is turning the Mennonites into an image of themselves, and setting the gaze of the camera on an intimate and forbidden universe thus creating a sense of shared embarrassment between the audience and the performers. Even without a sophisticated knowledge of Mennonite culture, we can't ignore the fact that acting in a film could have consequences for them, and we have to wonder their reasons for participating. So the negative space of the film, the other movie that plays simultaneously in the audience's head, is cluttered with conjectures, doubts and an extremely enhanced guilty voyeuristic pleasure created by the subversive power of a film that not only grants us access into a secluded realm, but also turns this traditionally introverted people into willing participants.

Reygadas believes characters should be constructed by the cinema and not created by the actors. His "method" is similar to that of Robert Bresson, for whom the presence of the actor is more important than the technical portrayal of a character. He doesn't believe that there is such a thing as acting natural because, to quote him again, "what we say and how we act is learned—no matter how natural we are, we are always acting the role of ourselves." For Reygadas, cinema should never be filmed theater (which he despises), nor "illustrated literature."

He doesn't believe in pretense or acting technique, but rather trusts in the Kulashov effect, creating sensations and ideas through juxtaposition of images. This way the viewer brings his own reactions to image sequences by-passing the need for explanations and actors pretending to portray emotions. Reygadas does not like rehearsing, he doesn't give his actors a screenplay, they don't know the story, psychological background, who or what they are, so they lack any knowledge of the feelings they should express. He only gives them spatial and temporal indications. To be sure that they have the correct timing, he sometimes ties strings to their legs to send them signals. In his search for strong emotions, he trusts the energy of his cast and he demands total trust from them.

Reygadas's influences can be traced from Andrei Tarkovsy and Roberto Rosselini to the Dardenne brothers and Bruno Dumont, but his fascination for the grotesque and the disturbing are also reminiscent of the Panic movement masters, Jodorowsky and Arrabal. His work evokes the films of Bergman and Kiarostami, filmmakers that Reygadas defines as "emotional," differentiating them from "intellectual" directors like Godard. For him, there is a simple difference between these two kinds of cinema: the former is self-contained while the latter depends on all sort of external and cultural references. There is nevertheless one huge shadow that hangs over *Stellet Licht*: Carl Theodor Dreyer's masterpiece, *Ordet* (Denmark, 1955). Dreyer's, film tells the story of a prosperous farmer, Morten Borgen, and his three sons, Mikkel who has renounced his faith, Andres who wants to marry a woman of a different religion and Johannes who has gone crazy from studying theology with too much fervor and believes he is the living Christ. The Borgens are put to a test when

Inger, Mikkel's wife and the source of energy, sexuality and warmth of the family, dies in childbirth. Johannes offers to bring her back, and he miraculously does so at the request of one of Inger's young daughters, the only member of the family who still has faith.

Both films deal with faith in provocative and disconcerting ways, rediscovering the primeval power of faith by rupturing its ties with organized religion. Both offer an ambiguous interpretation of the notion of faith, skeptical and reverential at the same time. Both reflect on the strangeness, fascination and irrationality of the belief in a supernatural power capable of ruling human destiny. Both employ light and shadows to represent the realms of the living and the dead with a painterly eye that recalls the Dutch masters of the 17th century and Velazquez. Both carry an immense spiritual weight and offer images of amazing beauty through an austere and severe *mise-en-scène*. Still they are very different films.

While Dreyer believes in the power of love as a force capable of transcending death, Reygadas has a more modest but perhaps more realistic proposition: "Peace is stronger than love." And he even leaves open the question if love could be the work of the devil. For its wonderful portrayal of spiritual struggle and sacrifice, temptation, love, guilt and forgiveness, *Stellet Licht* is as close to a masterpiece as one could imagine.

—Naief Yehya

#4

City of God

(Brazil, 2002):

Eight Years Later

The film *City of God*, which premiered in Britain and the U.S. in January 2003, was hailed by *Times* as one of the best 100 films in the history of cinema, amongst many other prestigious accolades. This comes as no surprise to those already familiar with its caliber that garnered it several major nominations and prizes. This film won a prize more valuable than a likely Academy Award by becoming a box-office hit with more than three million domestic viewers, and by provoking intense debates, nationally and internationally, around themes such as poverty, racism, and violence.

Cidade De Deus / City Of God (2002)
Images courtesy of O2 Filmes

Cidade De Deus / City Of God (2002)
Images courtesy of O2 Filmes

In what follows, I briefly survey the extent to which the groundbreaking *City of God*, by Fernando Meirelles, has pushed the frontiers of Brazil's and the world's film-making with reference to his successful follow up to the Brazilian film, the British production *The Constant Gardener* (2005), and to Danny Boyle's *Slumdog Millionaire* (U.K., 2008). The film's cinematic and social legacy in Brazil will be brought to bear with reference to the follow-up TV series *City of Men*.

The world's *favelas* as a cinematic sub-genre

City of God, which only flowed outwards when it was eventually distributed by Miramax, shares with its *Cinema Novo* predecessors one of the staples of Brazilian cinema, firm roots in the national reality. *Favelas* (Brazilian slums) started to be thematized by Brazilian Cinema in the mid-fifties with Nelson Pereira dos Santos's *Rio 40 Graus* [*Rio 40 Degrees*]. As Márcia P. Leite pointed out in 2003:

> . . . during the 1960s, especially with *Cinema Novo*—the movement that renewed Brazilian film production by dealing with national themes from a critical perspective and experimenting with unique forms and aesthetics—*favelas* were treated as one of the more perverse images of Brazilian urbanisation [. . .] Their focus was on the country's problems, at the time recognised as underdevelopment and misery.

Meirelles can be said to have updated *Cinema Novo's* agenda by moving away from the focus on underdevelopment and casting on the world's screens the brutal power dynamics of today's *favelas*: in the Brazilian case, the explosive, perverse process whereby drug dealers attract slum children to drugs and guns ("a sign of the victory of the market over the State reduced to impotence" as Schwarz argued in 2003). The camera and the sound technology of Meirelles's film hit the world's eyes and ears with the tragedy of dire poverty encountering drug trafficking. Exclusion as a social *locus* is rendered visible in its magnitude through his sophisticated use of technology.

Technology is indeed a point at which Fernando Meirelles departs radically from the hard-hitting films intended to "break the paradise of inertia of the public," and shock them into awareness through the use of rudimentary equipment and techniques associated with the doyen of *Cinema Novo* as Glauber Rocha discussed in 1995.

Meirelles's production further departs from mainstream cinema by thematizing the phenomenon of cityscapes of exclusion generated or amplified by the impact of global neoliberalism on the more vulnerable segments of so-called Third World economies. To the extent that neoliberalism amplifies the private space, frees the rich from the burden of contributing to the State's social functions, and frees the State from its redistributive role, it only deepens social inequality and exclusion. In this sense, *City of God* can be indeed a paramount example of how incoming cinemas locate cracks in Hollywood's prevailing ideology of triumphant capitalism. An updated social agenda, powerful cameras sweeping over Rio de Janeiro *favelas*, bravura editing, competent use of digital post-production technology, and world-wide distribution (i.e., Miramax) drew the world's attention to the burgeoning of quintessential sites of exclusion. In so doing, Meirelles projected to the world a new cinematic sub-genre: that of today's megalopolises' sprawling *favelas*.

The Constant Gardener: projecting the Kibera slum and de-performing stardom

Kibera, the largest slum in Sub-Saharan Africa—with a population of some 800,000 people beset by poverty, ill health and spreading AIDS and exploited by shadowy pharmaceutical companies—is at the very center of *The Constant Gardener* (2005). This adaptation of John Le Carré's homonymous novel picks up several patterns established by *City of God,* including the gritty realism of filming on location and naturalness in performance. *The Constant Gardener* may perhaps consolidate the view that mainstream cinema has been modified by the interaction and interplay with other incoming cinemas.

City of God's great experimentalism has filtered into innovative features of *The Constant Gardener.* This international film, Meirelles points out, had a much larger structure but in the end the processes were similar. De-interpretation and the use of little artificial lighting and its approach to rehearsing and filming have become actual filmmaking methods in *The Constant Gardener.* Meirelles achieved naturalness in the latter partly by carrying out rehearsals on almost all locations, which included northern Kenya, the country's slums, contrasting with the Jubilee Line in London, one of the epicenters of the global economy.

The effect of "controlled spontaneity" was achieved in *City of God* mostly through the technique of improvisation and all the filming methods devised by Meirelles to enhance the performance of non-professional actors who lacked formal training. Through improvisation, the actors grasped the mechanism of developing a situation out of a proposed conflict, without being given the dialogue. Meirelles would jot down the good ideas and interesting sentences and incorporate them into the script whose new draft they would start to go through. Conversely, *The Constant Gardener*, whilst reaffirming one of the staples of Hollywood, stardom, trained the renowned actors Rachel Weisz and Ralph Fiennes into "de-performing."

Slum Dog Millionaire: universalizing *City of God*'s film language

Ismail Xavier's reading of *City of God* can be eloquently adapted for *Slumdog Millionaire* (2008): it is another film in the commercial circuit that looks at life in extreme conditions and tries to show a road to liberation, while reflecting on media image of cinema as a means of salvation in the face of a social order of inequality, concentration of power and violence.

The good, the bad and the photographer (not the ugly as in the acclaimed Western) have been my metaphorical rendering of a society structured in terms of excluding binaries: the slum and the "asphalt" in *City of God*, but which allows a third (Buscapé or Rocket) to be empowered by knowledge of the power workings of the slum, by technology (his camera) and access to the media to break down barriers between the two worlds of the megalopolis.

Slumdog Millionaire's depiction of the urban ghetto connecting with the world at large via technology projects the megacity of Mumbai which is half made up of slums without clean water and sanitation. Both films depict the strategies developed by the economically and socially excluded in response to what Stuart Hall termed the "violence of non-recognition." Buscapé/Rocket positively integrates with the media world beyond the slum through photography and knowledge of the drug dealers. The media dimension finds a counterpart in Jamail's rise from rags to riches, on the strength of his intelligence and through positive representation in the media. In the brutal power dynamics in modern-day Mumbai, Jamail moves away from petty theft and similar improvisations of his way, such as pretending to be a guide, and prevails in the world through his wits.

In the initial scenes of *City of God*, the audience's look is met with the imploring eyes of a chicken—her legs tied, her fate sealed as suggested by the sound of a knife being sharpened. She breaks free of the strings round her legs and dashes off, believing that she is fleeing her fate—only to face the frantic chase of the armed gang under the command of Zé Pequeno (Li'l Zé). Walter Salles has ascribed a symbolic meaning to this traumatized chicken in a crossfire: she stands for so many Brazilians trapped in an unjust country.

The brief appearance, at the beginning of *Slumdog Millionaire*, of a chicken has afforded universal reach to Meirelles's icon which further points to new currencies being pursued by those trapped by poverty within today's slums. Authenticity in terms of filming on location and non-professional actors, the focus on children, the power of the media, dazzling cinematography are further elements of the film language used by Boyle that affirm Meirelles's groundbreaking establishment of the sub-genre of the sprawling *favela* in today's megalopolises.

City of God's production of social knowledge and awareness of racial inequalities

The actual *favela* Cidade de Deus (City of God), before Paulo Lins's novel which served as the basis for the film, was an open letter that no one cared to read. The problematic of this and other *favelas* in Brazil gained wide currency with Meirelles's *City of God*. Many from today's *favelas* now write and film themselves into being whilst important productions on the brutal power workings in the slums, such as Murat's *Maré, Nossa História de Amor* (2007) and Padilha's *Tropa de Elite* (2007) affirm the *favela* sub-genre.

Besides triggering social knowledge through the sub-genre, importantly, the growing screen space partly triggered by the participation of the largest black cast ever seen in a Brazilian film has interacted with and increased potential for a later major debate in Brazil, namely the assignment of quotas for black people who also lack social competitiveness to give them greater access to University.

The blacks in Brazil are indeed the most affected by the logic of capitalism's unequal and contradictory development which has hit the country hard and accentuated the differentiation between those who have economic, social and cultural capital access to the modes of production and can contract wage labour and those impoverished ones deprived of all sorts of capital.

The Cidade de Deus *favela* leader MV Bill, amongst others, has incorporated the screen into the debate, denouncing the racism of, for example, television programs that have mostly white actors. Others have denounced Brazilian television for framing the blacks within sports or dance or in subaltern roles (maids, drivers, and so on). Brazilian film, in turn, tends to present caricatures or stereotypes of blacks. One of the hurdles in fact faced by Meirelles was the relative dearth of black actors, paradoxically in a country whose population is approximately fifty percent black and which is reputed to have the second largest black population in the world, second only to Nigeria.

The class-race intersection punctuates the follow-up TV series *City of Men,* one episode of which, directed by Meirelles and Lund, provides ample screen space to blacks. The episode was first analyzed by Leandro Rocha Saraiva who underscored the impact of the film on television language, themes and patterns of beauty.

By a way of conclusion on a brief survey of eight years of repercussions of *City of God,* I quote Aaron Lorenz on the insight of the protagonists, Acerola and Laranjinha, into Brazil's race and class divides and the tension created "between a shared desire of the goals of utopian Freyreanism and the logic of racial discrimination":

> *Cidade dos Homens* shifts Freyre's vision away from an ideological state function and towards a more productive deployment for revindicating class and race equality [. . .] The narrators and protagonists frequently allude to racial divisions in Brazilian society as significant obstacles. In fact, attraction, fascination, and fear of the "other" form important thematic poles in the arc of the TV series evolution. Both playing Acerola and Laranjinha, or themselves, the two critique a hypocritical approach towards Freyrean *mestiçagem* that denies access to

work and education. Episodes like "a Coroa do Imperador," "Uólace e João Victor," and "Tem que ser agora," all explore the limits between racism and discrimination as well as the im/possibility of overcoming those boundaries. On the other end of the spectrum, there is a recuperation of a Freyreanism that provocatively imagines a single unified city. By "talking back," the two rehearse a radical Freyreanism that parodies notions of Freyrean sexual freedom and that substitutes a hypocritical notion of equality for a radicalized call for inclusion.

—Else R. P. Vieira

#5

Bus 174 / Ônibus 174

(Brazil, 2006)

As the first decade of the twenty-first century comes to a close, Brazil has emerged under the left-wing government of Lula da Silva as the economic engine of South America and a rising power in the global economy. At the same time, as an aspiring player in the new geopolitical system, it is striving to exert a leadership role on the international stage. However, the dazzling image of prosperity and modernity that Brazil has projected abroad, enabling it to secure the 2016 Olympic Games, sharply contrasts with

Ônibus 174 / Bus 174 (2002)
Image courtesy of Zazen Produções

the persistent socio-economic inequalities which continue to rend the national fabric and poison relationships between classes and ethnic groups. As Brazil's showcase to the world, the city of Rio de Janeiro explicitly embodies this dichotomy: on the one hand, it is a tourist mecca and a playground for a cosmopolitan upper class in possession of great wealth and a thriving middle class with access to the pleasures and distractions of late capitalism consumer society; on the other, its hillside slums (*favelas*) are home to a vast underclass stuck in endemic poverty, prey to violence, and prone to criminal behavior as a means for survival. In Rio, these two sharply contrasted universes carry on side by side in an uneasy co-existence based on denial, fear and coercion. On the occasions when these parallel worlds intersect, as in the flash-lightning raids of downtown hotels or shopping centers by hordes of gun-toting youth from the *favelas*, the economic and human costs of marginalization and exclusion burst forth with a stark, undeniable clarity.

Such a return of the repressed provided the inspiration for the documentary *Ônibus 174* co-directed by Jose Padilha and Felipe Lacerda. This award-winning film examines, from a variety of points of view, the circumstances surrounding and leading to the hijacking of a city bus in Rio. By means of this multiplicity of perspectives, the film's authors purported to shed light on the hijacker's background and motivations, thus countering the simplified, one-dimensional image of him served up by the mainstream media in their coverage of the event. In *Ônibus 174*, the hijacker, a young man of color from the *favela* of Rocinha named Sandro Rosa do Nascimento, is not depicted as a cardboard villain or a complete cipher; instead, he is presented as a complex human being whose actions cannot be untangled and divorced from the cumulus of forces and factors which shaped his past and induced him to undertake such a risky and ultimately fatal venture.

Ônibus 174 hit the international film festival circuit at a time of renewed interest in Brazilian cinema; coinciding with the successful commercial release of Fernando Meirelles's feature film *City of God, Ônibus 174* similarly presented an image of Rio steeped in social conflict and urban warfare, albeit without the flashy visual style of Meirelles's film. *Ônibus 174* performed very well at the box-office in Brazil, where it benefited from the event's notoriety, but its profitable run in foreign art houses and film societies is even more remarkable, given that few documentaries are ever distributed or find large audiences. Its success abroad attests to the gripping manner in which a story of local interest is retold and re-presented, managing to affect viewers beyond its national origins without losing its roots in a specific place and time.

The event that sparked the making of *Ônibus 174* took place on June 12, 2000. Unfolding over the course of approximately four hours and a half, the hijacking of bus 174 might have remained another local incident of violence, forgotten or ignored, had it not been for the television crews and radio reporters who approached the vehicle and almost from the very beginning provided minute-to minute live coverage of the hijacker's actions and words to a transfixed national audience. In the meantime, Rio's police force ineffectively stood by, hampered in its ability to intervene and defuse the situation by the state governor's politically motivated refusal to countenance bloodshed on national TV. Padilha, trapped in a gym adjacent to the crime scene, was among the millions of Brazilians who watched the entire event play out on TV. At the time, Padilha's sympathies rested squarely with the police and the hostages; Sandro was a mere nuisance whose foolhardy actions had brought the center of Rio to a halt, turning Padilha's day upside down, and thus needed to be subdued and/or eliminated. But reflecting later on the incident's resolution, Padilha, who was born into a wealthy family, became intrigued by Sandro's personality and decided to investigate his past in order to understand the reasons which compelled him to stage the hostage crisis.

The film's structure revolves around a series of interviews with relatives and acquaintances of Sandro as well as with some of the hostages and police officers present at the scene; the interviews are intercut with mostly unaired footage of the hijacking recorded by different TV stations. The picture of Sandro that emerges from Padilha and LaCerda's screenplay is that of a troubled, deeply scarred young man who hijacked bus 174 out of defiance as much as desperation. From his aunt Julieta, we learn that Sandro witnessed the murder of his pregnant mother when he was six years old, a trauma from which he apparently never recovered. In the aftermath, Sandro was taken in by his aunt but ran away and, after a stint in a reform school, mostly lived haphazardly on the streets of Rio, drifting into petty crime and the consumption of drugs. As social worker Yvonne Bezerra de Mello states in one of the interviews, Sandro's fate was unfortunately not that uncommon; the number of homeless children has grown exponentially in recent years—one figure claims an increase from about 1,200 children to over 20,000 in the decade spanning from 1993 to 2003—and has become a problem that neither the local authorities nor the institutions in charge of the children's welfare are capable of addressing, much less solving.

One of Sandro's throwaway lines during his exchanges with the police reveals another tragic facet of his childhood: his presence at the Candelaria church massacre of 1993. On July 23, seven homeless children, out of over sixty who were spending the night on the temple's steps, were murdered by a police squadron in a routine sweep of the downtown area; thirty-two survivors were subsequently killed over the years while several others disappeared without a trace. As the film tacitly suggests, the police's underground campaign of beatings, torture and assassination of street youth is one of the unspoken tactics deployed by the forces of law and order to deal with the epidemic of crime that plagues Rio. In *Ônibus 174*, Sandro's recollection of the Candelaria tragedy, of little resonance to an international audience, is charged with enormous weight if we consider the fraught relationships between Rio's poor and the police, who implicitly act at the behest of the upper classes' socio-economic interests and concern for property and personal safety. In this context, Sandro's offhand reference to being a Candelaria survivor becomes a taunt directed at the officers outside, as much a defiant reassertion of his personhood as a denunciation of the state-endorsed violence which has engulfed him since an early age.

One of the film's more shocking sequences involves a visit to the jail where Sandro was once incarcerated for theft. Interviews with some of the inmates, whose identities are masked through a kind of solarization effect, unveil the sordid, quasi-inhuman conditions in which the prisoners are forced to live: squalor, overcrowding, lack of medical attention, physical abuse, and the constant threat of deadly violence. It is not surprising then, as one of the inmates points out, that those who exit the jail would prefer to die than ever return to what they describe as a "living hell." Their words not only offer an indictment of Brazil's penal system but go as far as condemning the entire society for its oblivious attitude. It is likely that Sandro, too, preferred death over incarceration and was at least conscious of the possibility that he might not leave the bus alive, in which case the hijacking takes on the guise of a suicide mission. Either way, Sandro took advantage of the presence of the cameras to turn the stranded bus into a sort of improvised soapbox from which, in a disconnected series of rants and violent gestures, he asserted his right to be heard and taken seriously.

If throughout his life Sandro had been made to feel powerless, the gun in his hand granted him a degree of previously denied power. If his being and suffering had been rendered invisible to his fellow Brazilians, the presence of the media had suddenly put the spotlight on his plight, presenting an entire nation with the distressing spectacle of an angry, drug-addled outcast uttering a few uncomfortable truths about Brazil's social contract and, in the process, exposing the underbelly of Brazil's economic miracle for all to see. Throughout the film, Sandro displays flashes of self-awareness that reveal an understanding of his predicament as one thoroughly mediated by the cameras trained upon his body. Referring perhaps to the public's current fascination with reality television—where the boundaries between fiction and documentary, the staged and the authentic are purposefully blurred—and action pictures, Sandro at one point shouts out through the bus's window: "This isn't a movie, this is the real thing." While Sandro's declaration questions the media's tendency to turn even an act of random violence arising from existential despair into pure entertainment—coverage of the hijacking earned television stations such as Globo some of their highest ratings of the year—it also interrogates the very core of the documentary practice, with its claims for truthfulness and transparency, thus providing a self-reflexive commentary on Padilha and Lacerda's own film.

Ônibus 174 also allots time to the thoughts of a few female hostages on their ordeal and they, too, reflect back on Sandro's posturing as kind of theater of violence intended to instill fear and reap certain results. Janaina, one of the hostages states that, as the hijacking dragged on, a certain complicity between Sandro and the bus's passengers began to develop, if only as a strategy to ensure their own survival, leading them to collaborate to a certain extent in the "spectacularization" of their own victimizing. Of course, the uncertainty over Sandro's mental state made things utterly unpredictable. When he finally decided to step out of the bus after several tense hours, Sandro left accompanied by one of the hostages, Geísa, held at gunpoint as a shield against police fire. By this point, the BOPE, a SWAT-like unit, had arrived on the scene and encircled the bus. The tragedy that ensued is re-played in the film in slow motion using footage shot from different angles, which adds to the suspenseful build-up. As Sandro advanced towards the BOPE's chief, Captain Batista, standing just a few meters away, a young agent stepped up behind the hijacker and fired two shots directed at him, missing his target; as he fell to the ground, Sandro, in turn, shot Geísa dead. Trying to prevent a lynching by an angry mob that rushed to the site of the shooting, four police officers forcibly dragged Sandro into a van, where he died of suffocation on the way to the police station. As professor Amy Villarejo has argued, Sandro managed to stay alive as long as he remained in the public eye, but died as soon as the absence of cameras rendered him invisible again and vulnerable to state repression. In the ensuing investigation, all four officers were acquitted. However, in the aftermath of criticism directed at the police's mismanagement of the incident, *Ônibus 174* is apparently screened today in Brazil's police academies as part of their training program.

In the end, viewers who are willing to put their prejudices aside are placed in the position of having to decide whether another outcome might have been possible and, more importantly, whether the all-around institutional failure depicted in the film can be redressed so that fewer Sandros are compelled to counter their lack of prospects with acts of violence. *Ônibus 174* stirred considerable discussion in Brazil, although its reception paled in comparison to the intense controversy unleashed by Padilha's follow-up film, *Tropa de elite* (*Elite Squad*, 2007), a fictional account of the brutal doings of a BOPE team in their ruthless battle against drug dealers and slum dwellers. Furthermore, the resonance of Sandro's story spawned a fiction film, *Ultima Parada 174* (*Last Stop 174*, 2008), directed by veteran filmmaker Bruno Barreto. Like Barreto, Meirelles and Hector Babenco, whose *Pixote* (1981) was a seminal look at the plight of Rio's street children, Padilha has leveraged the critical success of his first films into a transnational career. Lured to Hollywood to work on English-language projects, Padilha nevertheless remains committed to working in his country's film industry and has plans to finish his informal trilogy on Brazil's dysfunctional society with a film about the corruption permeating its political system.

—Gerard Dapena

Y Tu Mamá También (2001)
Images courtesy of IFC Films

#6

Y Tu Mamá También

(Mexico, 2001)

The lights went down in the theater and the screen lit up with Diego Luna's bare, larger-than-life pumping buttocks. Having just introduced the film at a retrospective of Mexico cinema and explained rather earnestly its political and cultural significance eight years after its release, I realized that I had forgotten this provocative beginning (and maybe ought to have warned the startled 90-something woman in the back row). But there could be no other beginning. *Y Tu Mamá También*'s opening scene—followed by a parallel scene introducing Gael García Bernal's naked backside—of clumsy, late-adolescent sex sets up perfectly the tensions that propel this male-fantasy road movie through to the unexpected and controversial climax that served to generate a viral marketing campaign.

The film's title, uttered almost exclusively in Spanish by its endless number of English-speaking fans, literally translates as "And Your Mother, Too" and references the central conflict. The story begins with the fart jokes, poolside masturbation, and drug-enhanced summer escapades of two playful yet self-absorbed best friends from different social classes as they wrap up their blissful high school life. With instigation from an attractive older woman, the boys' camaraderie turns quickly to petty bickering, then macho rivalry, and eventually erupts in a confessional of mutual betrayal: each admits to having slept with the other's girlfriend, then lists a number of other conquests, jokingly ending with "your mother."

But the loaded cultural meaning of so profane a violation, even in jest, embodies the ambiguities of this story about Mexico's sexual, social, and political coming of age nearly two centuries after its declared independence.

The genre conventions of the film combine the road movie's tourist camera and the buddy movie's male antics with the risqué pleasures of Mexico's contemporary sex comedies, as the two boys, Julio (García Bernal) and Tenoch (Luna), traverse their native land to take the visiting Spanish beauty, Luisa (Maribel Verdú), from the capital city to the coast. Created by a real-life buddy team of director Alfonso Cuarón and his brother Carlos, *Y Tu Mamá También* was shot in 1999, just before the historic elections in which presidential candidate Vicente Fox and the National Action Party (PAN) would overturn the 71-year reign of the Institutional Revolutionary Party (PRI). It was released in June 2001, one year after the election outcome and the release of *Amores Perros* had upset Mexico's political and cultural stases, respectively, both with campaigns for radical change. Its ample gestation time for marketing resulted in one of the biggest box-office openings in the history of Mexican cinema: coming home from premiering in Cannes, the film took in $2.2 million in its first week. After its U.S. theatrical release in 2002 by IFC and Good Machine, it went on to win the Independent Spirit Award for Best Foreign Film and Best Picture from the Los Angeles Film Critics.

While its casting of now heartthrob García Bernal allowed it to ride the wake of *Amores Perros*'s publicity, the lighter tone helped to avoid the common critiques made by audiences that Mexican cinema was too obsessed with violence and poverty. And yet *Y Tu Mamá También*'s allusions to this monumental historical political shift at the break of the new millennium, as well as to Mexico's consistently divisive socioeconomic hierarchies, were not only made explicit through the contrasting characters and landscapes, but are thrust into relief by the film's visual and narrative mechanisms. The most noticeable of these mechanisms is the use of an abrupt, intrusive omniscient narrator, whose voice freezes the diegetic audio track to explain the political and/or social significance of the scene, often with minor details related to characters' personal histories, career choices, or minor foibles. What runs constant through the seemingly arbitrary comments is that they seem to foreshadow the dramatic conflict of betrayal and the final scene's conclusion that a friendship across

Y Tu Mamá También (2001)
Images courtesy of IFC Films

class boundaries is ultimately unsustainable. For example, early in the film the boys' interaction with their girlfriends, who are leaving for a summer abroad, is enhanced by a commentary that characterizes each of the girls' parents by their profession and remarks on how each reacts with relative amounts of conservatism or skepticism to their daughter's love life. Upping the thematic gravity, the narrator begins to explain the social contradictions of the urban and rural landscapes with details that underscore the young protagonists' obliviousness to their surroundings. Like the dramatic centerpiece of contingent actions and colliding destinies of *Amores Perros* (and that of numerous other independent films of the late-century era), two crucial voiceover interruptions in *Y Tu Mamá También* focus on automobile accidents. First, when Julio and Tenoch are stuck in traffic and assume it is due to a political protest, we discover that it is in fact a fatal accident of a bus striking a pedestrian who crossed a busy thoroughfare to get to work, a clear commentary on the less-than-accommodating infrastructure of Mexico's more industrial and less affluent zones. Later, the same voiceover explains that a curve in the road had been the sight of a fatal accident ten years prior, a fact that informs the foreign viewer of the macabre meaning behind the decorative crosses that dot the roadside throughout the film. Towards the end of the film, the narrator explains in indisputable terms the negative impact of Mexico's opening to neoliberal economic policies on traditional, local industries, such as fishing. The cinematography manages to reproduce the observational but not unbiased tone of the voiceover by depending almost exclusively on a handheld camera, which is positioned in a series of dramatically low or high angles that switch between pursuing the characters' movement in close proximity or reframing them with a distant, voyeuristic point of view using windows and other architectural thresholds. This complex layering of images and sounds, both of whose artistic style embrace their medium's ability to blur the subjective/objective boundary, results in a repeated return to the viewer's contradictory position of being complicit in a celebration of sexual adventure and debauchery while lamenting, if not condemning, the tragic undertones that the characters ignore.

Though the film's stylization is subtler than that of its cinematic contemporaries, it is sufficient to fit it squarely into the aesthetic trends occurring throughout Latin America at this time. And like other productions, aesthetic and economic factors moved in tandem. Cuarón chose to secure private financing rather than pursue the bureaucratic funding channels of the Mexican Film Institute (IMCINE). With the upstart company Producciones Anhelo, underwritten by corporate millionaire Jorge Vergara, he followed a production model relatively new to Mexico, which included such seemingly trivial details as a music soundtrack. But it was precisely this element that allowed Anhelo to take advantage of its corporate affiliates and engage in synergistic marketing strategies that focused on the booming youth consumer market. While this model presented itself as a new formula based on artistic innovation and international appeal, and breaking the traditions of a nationalistic of the state cinema, the end product did not forego the value of its geographic origins. This unofficial co-production between Spain and Mexico brings its own dose of nationalism, such as using the last names of the principal characters to reference important figures in the Mexican

Revolution (Zapata, Carranza, Madero) and its independence from Spain (Iturbide, Morelos). The last name of the Spanish seductress, Cortés, is that of the Spanish conquistador who invaded Mexico in the 16th century. Similar winks to the film's national audience include a certain novelty in the writing and performance of dialogues, chock full of *chilango* slang. The young characters mumble and whisper their interjections and obscenities through mouthfuls of food, alcohol, and smoke, offering a relative amount of realism compared to the histrionics of Mexico's traditional melodrama and the melodically exaggerated accents of its popular film heroes.

Perhaps what is now most notable about this production is what it has done for its participants' international recognition and subsequent careers. *Y Tu Mamá También* was Alfonso Cuarón's homecoming film after years in Hollywood (*The Little Princess* [1995], *Great Expectations* [1998]), and yet it proved more effective than anything prior in launching his transnational status, as the director of *Harry Potter and the Prisoner of Azkaban* (2004) and the English-language sci-fi production *Children of Men* (2006). Luna and García Bernal did not let their off-screen partnership come to an end, joining together to create the production and distribution company Canana while also pursuing independent careers. Luna made a handful of domestic hits before being offered supporting roles in Harmony Kornine's *Mister Lonely* (2007) and Gus Van Sant's *Milk* (2008). He debuted as director with the documentary *J. C. Chávez* (2007), and more recently directed his first narrative feature, *Abel* (2010), which premiered at the Sundance Film Festival. After headlining Mexico's follow-up cinematic scandal, *The Crime of Father Amaro* (2002) by Carlos Carrera, García Bernal took lead roles in Walter Salles's *The Motorcycle Diaries* (2004), Pedro Almodovar's *Bad Education* (2004), Michel Gondry's *The Science of Sleep* (2006), followed shortly after by his directorial debut, *Deficit* (2006). The duo reunited as actors in 2008 to make screenwriter Carlos Cuarón's directorial debut, *Rudo y Cursi*, a comedy about two brothers whose soccer stardom sets them up as each other's worst rival. Actress Maribel Verdú worked with Guillermo del Toro in *Pan's Labyrinth* (2006), which earned her two best-actress awards and several nominations.

If the film itself marks a new dawn for Mexican cinema (and this is still under debate), the story seems to indicate a two-steps-forward/one-step-back attitude towards social progress. The narration at the end of the film makes clear that the course of Julio and Tenoch's friendship, which ends after their shared sexual encounter, runs parallel to the nation's political transition. Both mark the end of an era with a moment of idealism, in what at first seems to be a clean break from the historical stagnancy of corruption and authoritarianism and the social repression of *machismo* and homophobia; yet in fact, it is not much of a break at all, as the new ruling party happened to be the most conservative of all and the post-election enthusiasm returned quickly to apathy. After watching the film from beginning to end, the viewer must choose what he or she wants to remember: the carefree, naked bodies who for an instant flee the hypocrisy of their imposed gender and class identities; or the young men who sit quiet and awkward in a diner, knowing that summer is over and the cruel reality of their new phase of life is just beginning.

—Misha Maclaird

Whisky (2004)
Image courtesy of the Global Film Initiative

#7

Whisky

(Uruguay, 2004)

Whisky co-directed by (the late) Juan Pablo Rebella and Pablo Stoll is the second feature by this Uruguayan thirty-something duo. It is a simple, understated film that finds great humor and pathos in documenting what many may see as the banal routines of everyday life, but what we could also call the microhistories that structure our lives.

The film was very well received by critics and in international film festivals. The screenplay was honored with the Sundance-NHK International Filmmakers Award for Latin America, and the finished film went on to win accolades, most notably the Jury Award at the Cannes Film Festival (Un Certain Regard), followed by the Tokyo Gran Prix at the Tokyo International Film Festival, the Golden Coral at the Havana Film Festival, and prizes for the best Latin American film at both Mexico's Ariel Awards and Spain's Goya Awards. Moreover, it was selected by Uruguay to represent the country in the best foreign film category at the Oscars.

Filming *Whisky* took two months and was a labor of love. In the film's press book, directors Rebella and Stoll described the process: "It is extremely difficult to produce a film in Uruguay . . . But in Uruguay it is difficult to produce anything at all." Uruguay, a country of three million people, has difficulty sustaining a film industry without the support of other, wealthier nations to co-finance films. In addition to monetary support from the Uruguayan film fund FONA, the film received co-production funds from Argentina, Spain, and Germany.

Rebella and Stoll splashed on to the international film scene in 2001 with their first feature: the low budget, off-the-wall, black and white *25 Watts*. Produced for a mere $200,000, the film won, most notably, the Tiger Award at the Rotterdam film festival and the FIPRESCI prize at the Buenos Aires International Festival of Independent Cinema "for injecting humor, visual energy and delightful dialogue into the 'Slacker' movie formula."

The directors are part of a new generation of Uruguayan filmmakers who are telling more intimate stories than those of their counterparts from the 60s–70s who formed part of the militantly political New Latin American Cinema Movement (most exemplified in the Uruguayan context by Mario Hendler). Their cinematic style has been compared to *auteurs* such as Jim Jarmusch, in particular his early work, and Aki Kaurismaki. Both born in 1974, Rebella and Stoll met while studying social communications at the Catholic university in Montevideo and have worked together as co-writers/directors until Rebella met an untimely death in 2006.

Whisky opens by examining the mundane quotidian practices of a sixty-something sock factory owner, Jacobo Koller (Andrés Pazos), who is depicted in his daily morning ritual drinking morning coffee, silently, in a darkened café before driving to his office. He is greeted outside the corrugated metal garage door daily by his longtime, faithful employee, Marta (Mirella Pascual). Argentine critic Diego Batlle for the newspaper *La Nación* posits that while this film displays universal traits such as loneliness and impossibility of communication, it also depicts a very authentic and accurate picture of Montevideo as a deteriorating city, with its "social decay which is hardly perceptible but persistently there . . . a mix of nobility, nostalgia, dignity and pathos which defines ordinary people in the grey and monotonous life of the capital city."

We see the rehearsed and tired exchanges that occur day after day, until the occasion of Jacobo's mother's tombstone unveiling, the *matzeveh* (which occurs one year after burial in the Jewish faith). For this auspicious event, Jacobo's younger brother Herman (Jorge Bolani), who owns a modern and more successful sock factory in Brazil, flies to Montevideo for the ritual ceremony after a twenty year absence.

Jacobo, a consummate bachelor, asks Marta if she will pose as his wife in order to give his brother a better impression of him. Marta, ever the dutiful factotum, agrees. Paying ever attention to detail, she suggests they stage false wedding pictures, hence prompting them to pose for the camera and exclaim, "Whisky!" (the Spanish version of saying "cheese").

The understated rivalry between Jacobo and Herman is teeming below the surface, stemming in part from the resentment harbored by Jacobo after his sacrifice of nursing their ailing mother until her death. Herman, in contrast, did not so much as send financial assistance or attend the funeral. This film cleverly demonstrates how the brothers are polar opposites so that it is no wonder they have not communicated in decades. Indeed, they are foils: Jacobo is taciturn, stoic, if not a bit curmudgeonly, in contrast to Herman, an upbeat, gregarious, flirtatious, and clearly more self-assured counterpart. Despite their differences, however, there are amusing parts of the film showing how in fact they have more common traits befitting brothers than one might expect. For example, in two different instances, the brothers unknowingly exchange the same gifts with each other, to droll effect.

One of the stylistic choices made by the directors was the use of the static camera. A deliberate choice was made not to use tilts, pans or zooms. Therefore, if one character was taller than another (as demonstrated by Jacobo and Marta), there is a body part, such as Jacobo's head, that is often cut off from our view. This form of framing adds a quirky, disjointed effect to the film, but one to great effect as minimalism and asymmetry somehow work in tandem here.

When the three protagonists embark on a road trip to the Uruguayan seaside town of Piriápolis in Jacobo's run-down car, the *mise*-en-*scène* shifts from the drab, ordinary, industrial part of Montevideo to a resort town symbolizing the Koller brothers' lost youth. The hotel setting, albeit a bit outdated, allows the trio to meet young, Argentine newlyweds (played by real-life couple, actors Daniel Hendler and Ana Katz) and to spend leisure time sipping cocktails at a deserted and somewhat depressing karaoke bar. This change of environment allows Marta a chance to be on vacation, to dress more formally and even to flirt and gain the attention of Herman—something that Jacobo does not have the will or desire to give her. This newly felt attention, despite mainly serving as a form of unspoken competition between the two brothers, has a transformative effect on Marta. It is as if she is experiencing a new lease on life, creating a sparkle in her eye that was not there before. This *joie de vivre* sets off some interesting dialogue and one in which makes her a more lively and refreshingly (somewhat) childish character. Near the end of the film there is an exchange of a written note from Marta to Herman before he departs to Brazil, and back to a possibly hum drum life with his wife and children. The audience is never told what the note says or what becomes of Marta at the film's end; we only sense that she is in pursuit of more fulfilling life opportunities.

The film's major strength is Marta's well-developed character arc, but also Jacobo's sensitization. The actors fit the roles like gloves. Despite it being about a middle-aged group of characters, the film's beauty is that resignation and isolation is portrayed by them in clear, albeit often unspoken ways, in a non-age-specific manner. In fact, the directors noted, again in the press book, that: "When we wrote the script, we started to realize that perhaps these characters were not much different from ourselves. That we were not altogether so far from these three types of loneliness." Sadly, this film collaboration was to be Juan Pablo Rebella's last. In 2006, Rebella ended his life prematurely, thus truncating their short-lived, but extremely lauded directorial careers. Pablo Stoll continues directing films, his most recent being *Hiroshima* (2009) a film he dedicated to his late directing partner.

—Tamara L. Falicov

La mujer sin cabeza / The Headless Woman (2008)
Images courtesy of Strand Releasing

#8

They and the Others, in a Country Gone Mad:

The Headless Woman

(Argentina, 2008)

Lucrecia Martel's third feature film is completely consistent with her previous work. It's a film of moods, hints and intimations. Highly complex, it evades all possibility of certainty. Once again, the plot's turning point is a pretext, although in this case it may be more important than in her previous films. It's an excuse to depict feminine psychology, and to show that Martel is a lucid observer of her province's society—of all its social, traditional and class features, as well as its speech and customs—and, by means of this microcosm, of the whole country and its history.

The anecdote itself could be dispensed with (and not because it is well known): a woman hits something or someone on the highway, and enters an altered state of consciousness. Meanwhile, all around her a network of complicity hides what she did.

Martel, it has been repeatedly said, is a creator of mood. As in *La Ciénaga*, from the very first scene there is an ominous mood of something brewing, of imminent danger. Three indigenous boys and a dog are recklessly playing in an open space beside a nearly deserted highway. Cut to a group of middle-class women and children, who are about to leave after a meeting in an enclosed space which we do not see, probably a club. The smallest of the children plays inside a car, also an enclosed space. "You'll run out of air," Verónica, the protagonist, tells him. She leaves. The film's beginning, cut into two scenes, creates a feeling of menace, suggests the imminence of catastrophe.

When the accident takes place on the lonely highway, the camera frames Verónica from the empty passenger seat. As she drives, she turns to answer her cellphone, and the car runs hard over something. Verónica knocks her head against the roof of the car, but recovers and stops the vehicle. She starts to turn to look behind her, but finally does not. She picks up her dark glasses and puts them on. Her face has become hardened. Her body, sweating and breathing fast, expresses her inner tension. She starts the car and goes on her way, not looking back.

A storm is coming. The whole scene, filmed in one continuous shot, is masterful. Only after this scene do we see the car driving away from a dead dog lying on the highway.

From that point on, the camera will persistently follow and keep a close distance from Verónica: in angled profiles from behind her back, in imbalanced close-ups, and using depth-of-field to simultaneously stage different actions, showing background characters out of focus. Ruptures in the narrative, lack of information, and breaks in the cause-effect relationship could be related to the shock that Verónica has suffered. Now, the cracks in everyday banality, which are usually so well camouflaged, become visible. It is possible that Verónica is experiencing a sudden clarity regarding the world around her.

Verónica is a blonde diva admired in her provincial society. This is a Creole society that retains much of feudalism, a matriarchal structure filled with endogamy, incest—latent or consummated—youthful homosexuality, degraded men, the bed as a place of family reunion, the significant importance of the corporeal. It is the society of Salta to which Martel belonged, the only place where she has filmed so far and whose landscape she has depicted in her film triptych.

In this society where patriarchy and superstitious religion persist, there is a system of almost feudal servitude, where indigenous women take on the thankless duties of the lords and solve their problems for them, where young boys are always on hand for all kinds of chores. These are the characters that surround Verónica, who are with her in her life and in the film. Verónica enjoys the privileges of her class: she has two assistants in her dentist's office, two maids in her home, a masseuse who attends to her in her own bedroom, a gardener, a boy who washes her car, etc.

Martel chooses a particular manner of cutting things out from reality, and she does this in all instances of the film: in the fragmentation of bodies, the constant reframing of shots, the use of ellipses and the out-of-field, the lack of explanations. She insists on cutting out the figure of the protagonist: the top of her head is always left above frame, and her figure near the edge of the frame, rarely in the center.

They—Verónica, her husband, her cousins—seem not to notice the others. If *La Ciénaga* developed a relationship of attraction-rejection between the social classes, here the protagonist and those who surround her are disconnected from a social reality that they find alien. Though they share common spaces and situations—and even a glass with water, in an elaborate long take—they remain dissociated, as if living in different wavelengths.

One of the characters seems more perceptive than the rest: Lala, the matriarch confined to her bed—like

Mecha in *La Ciénaga*—who lives in a sort of lucid senile dementia. It is Lala who notices that the protagonist is now different, that her voice has changed. She says to Verónica, "Ghosts. The house is filled with them. Don't look at them, and they'll go away," while in the background, the shadowy figure of a boy—evocative of the accident—walks out of frame. A great moment of artistic culmination for María Vaner, who plays Lala.

In an essential moment, Verónica drops her autistic silence and clearly and dispassionately tells her husband that she thinks she has killed someone on the highway. From that moment on, the network of men who surround her—husband, brother, cousin-lover (lawyers, doctors, police officers)—denies that possibility. They all attempt to relieve her of her burden.

Everyone employs the phrase, so frequent in Argentina: "*No pasa nada.*" (Literally, "Nothing is happening" but more accurately, "There's no problem here.") At this point, the politic parable alluding to the recent past of the last dictatorship becomes obvious. Just like in those times, the victim is absent, unseen. Verónica didn't see a victim, but everyone knows that a boy has disappeared. As in those times, the body social adopts a complicit silence, avoids discussing what is happening or the seriousness of events. From the first moment, Verónica has not assumed responsibility for her acts, and does not take charge of what she has unwittingly caused. She didn't even look at what she ran over.

Or maybe she didn't kill the boy. We only saw a dog. Everything adds to vague suggestions, ambiguities. Uncertainty reigns—the film refuses to provide certainty, in one sense or the other, although the clues tend to point out that Verónica is guilty.

But there is always a visual element that evokes the accident: from the moment the accident takes place, we can see prints of children's hands on the car window. We know they were left there by the children who were playing in the car in the previous scene, yet they also suggest the possible victim. In another shot, the traces of the accident are different: an error in continuity that suggests it has been "planted" as if it were false evidence. At the hospital, Verónica sees a woman being held in custody, escorted by a police officer. Verónica knows she could very well find herself in the same position. Back at her home, her husband brings in an animal that he killed hunting, and the presence of that other prey, dead on the kitchen table, reinforces the feeling of the macabre. When Verónica goes to her car, she sees the broken headlight as a consequence of the crash. Back at the club, the barking of dogs, the sound of glass breaking, and seeing a boy lying on the ground at a soccer field, alter Verónica so much that she bursts into tears and hugs a worker who was making repairs outside the restroom—a visible and involuntary manifestation of her tribulations, as she veers on the brink of collapse. A striking contrast in skin color and attitude: the lady, the servant. Time and time again Verónica returns to the place where the disappeared boy used to work, to the neighborhood where his family lives. She searches for news of his death in the newspaper, but hides her interest in the issue, tenaciously clinging to her emotional disconnection, always with her head divided.

Around her, people don't talk about, inform or acknowledge what happened—they hide it, mask it, just like when they repair her car in a different city. An obvious parallel with the actions of a great part of the population, specially that specific social class during the last dictatorship. "What should I do? What do I have to do?" Verónica asks her brother, a dentist like her. "Sleep," he answers. Verónica removes herself from responsibility and leaves the handling of her problem to the men. As in political history, the elaborate construction of a fictitious reality hides from us, from Verónica and from the audience, the knowledge of what really happened. This is the way that History is written and social conscience is built. By means of individual choices, of lack of responsibility for personal actions, the network acts as a whole, and what began individually becomes collective. From politics to a parable of ethics: Martel has repeatedly stated that the film not only attempts to deal with the history of self-repression of the population during the dictatorship when many people refused to acknowledge what was happening or chose not to report on the crimes committed against citizens, but that it also attempts to denounce the present-day situation of fractured social relations, the subjugation of the poorest people in the country, the refusal of the higher classes to acknowledge that the others are in the gutter. The others are fading into the background, out of focus, and run the risk of being left out of the social structure. The mechanism to ignore this reality is the same that negated the reality of the seventies. This is the reason why Martel employs music from that decade, always diegetically, in this present-day story.

Paradoxically, some have inadvertently criticized the film because there's "nothing going on" in it, despite the many events and the richness of meaning. Martel steers away from conventional, redundant and explanatory filmmaking, and refuses to tie the strings of the plot. Her ambiguity opens enigmas, suggests worlds, and does not provide answers; it demands from the viewer an intelligent and active attitude to access multiple readings.

Perhaps certain critics' first rejection of the film could be explained by the difficulty in identifying with the protagonist or with any of the characters; even though the director's camera work attempts to give the audience the feeling of being inside the scene, of being part of the action, as if the camera itself were one of the characters. A character witness to the action, like an observer, always impartial, who does not incur moral judgment.

With only three films to her name, Lucrecia Martel reveals herself as a master of observation and representation of class hierarchy in Argentine society, as well as of feminine psychology. *The Headless Woman* has confirmed Martel as the most intelligent, original and subtle director in contemporary Argentine cinema.

—Josefina Sartora

La niña santa / The Holy Girl (2004)
Images courtesy of Lita Stantic Producciones

#9

The Holy Girl

(Argentina, 2004)

Lucrecia Martel's filmmaking possesses a forcefulness that resembles a river with several currents flowing side-by-side and, once in a while, crossing into each others' paths. To call it a crosscurrent, however, would not describe its actual movements, which can be nearly imperceptible as these currents overlap or occasionally intertwine to the point of confluence. Her films are inhabited by different instants of narrative, each one looking to overpower what's happening before our eyes. Discussing Martel's cinema involves a willingness to let yourself drift along these currents, while at the same time making a constant effort to decipher an environment often laden with multiple possibilities.

Martel has a way of presenting a story's actions in an elliptical and sensory-rich manner, a device through which the narrative vectors and elements of plot, rather than figuring prominently, are instead whispered or even insinuated. Her films provoke a strange or disorienting effect, because the Argentine director somehow establishes her own unique, order of things. She tackles tired film genres from the point of view of a craftsman, redesigning them to unveil something original and demanding. Her ability to do this really becomes clear with her second feature, *The Holy Girl*, a grand take on adolescence, bathed in sexual desire and religious belief. At first glance, it may remind one of a love triangle (just barely), a psychological thriller (minimally), and, at times, a comedy of errors (only slightly). To unequivocally call it a thriller or farce, however, is as erroneous as stating that *Turning Gate* (South Korea, 2002), by Hong Sang-soo, is a romantic comedy. Martel's film takes certain elements from these familiar formulas and gives them a completely distinct meaning—so distinct that they are barely recognizable. If there is a love triangle to be had, it runs counter to the aggressive trope: it is passive, it thrives through its omissions, and it relies on what the protagonists don't know, rather than on the things they do.

As a film about the confusing and exploratory stage of adolescence, *The Holy Girl* presents that rare occasion when the libido, curiosity, and the search for religion (in a notoriously Catholic society like that in Argentina) can all somehow work in concert. It all starts with an overwhelming shot in which Amalia (María Alché) and Josefina (Julieta Zylberberg) sing a religious hymn along with their classmates. The two of them have faces that could belong to an angel and a devil. They have expressions of agony and ecstasy, pain and pleasure, two sides to a coin—the key on which this ambiguous current of desires, eroticism, and mysticism resonates throughout the film. Their teacher Inés (Mía Maestro) tells them to answer God's call—an invitation from Him to all who can save and be saved—urging them to immediately find their calling within His Divine Plan. Martel wastes no time and cuts to an event hall at a hotel, where a medical conference is getting underway. Helena (Mercedes Morán), who is Amalia's mother and the owner of the hotel, is seated. No more than a few seconds pass and she is told that her ex-husband, Manuel, is expecting twins with his new partner. In two blows, the director has put the central problems of the film on the table: a young girl trying to answer God's call—i.e., finding holiness, or her interpretation of it—and her mother, who finds herself in the midst of a midlife crisis, trying to fill a hole in her life. The laconic Dr. Jano, a participant in the medical conference, arrives at the hotel and will transform into the unlikely object of salvation for both of them: mystical in one case, emotional in the other. These first ten minutes are masterful because Martel also establishes her own rules for the game. The conflict has been outlined, but the fog that descends is thick. We don't know exactly where we are physically (i.e., in Salta, in the north of Argentina), we only have a vague idea of who the characters are and what their relationships to each other, and truthfully, this impression is drawn out, as the director chooses this alternative to pave the way on which the key questions in the film will roll throughout.

This code, set up in the film's opening, also reveals the manner in which Martel blends formal elements. It isn't

La niña santa / The Holy Girl (2004)
Images courtesy of Lita Stantic Producciones

only apparent in the tension that emerges from every shot—her stylized compositions, the framing that leaves little room in the visual field, people with their backs turned, the feeling of confinement, or the indoor lighting—but in the very sound. It's fascinating to see how the director fuels the film with noises and sounds that come from the surrounding reality. For example, when the girls' calling is set up, one hears music that recalls classic suspense films. The strange melody, easily mistaken for a cliché musical score, however, emerges from the street below and is played on a Theremin—an unconventional, musical instrument whose sounds are made by moving one's hands, which are held some distance apart from it. The resonance of the instrument and the melodies it plays—some quite popular—shape a large part of the film's soundtrack and accompany many of its key moments, like the famous scene in which Dr. Jano approaches Amalia from behind, in the middle of a crowd, and rubs his crotch against her. With this same *modus operandi*, other scenes are accompanied by the sound of a microphone being connected, the endless running of water in a heated pool, or the murmur of people in the distance.

Taking note of the elaborate pattern that emerges in this film, it is evident that behind it all, there must be someone working sensitively and intuitively. In an interview I conducted with Martel regarding *The Headless Woman* (2008), she commented that plot in her films is almost like a residue left behind by a sequence of little events that build up, as opposed to the majority of films, where plot drives them. She said that her interest lies in sharing with the audience the kinds of situations where even she is unsure of the consequences: a process that emerges without need for a master plan, unlike a chess game. During that conversation, we delved into her command of sound design. She explained it as her consistent point of departure, and that in general, she has a clear idea of the sound she wants, which then results in an easier time writing. She even joked that it's cheaper to film if one has this system of working, because once she has the sound concept for the film, she ends up shooting less.

Without a doubt, there's an organic density to Martel's work, an attribute held by directors with a unique signature. It's impossible to separate the *mise-en-scène* from the story, to the point that the director's decisions appear to be the most logical ones for the idea being conveyed. While Amalia looks to atone for Dr. Jano's sins for his inappropriate contact, and Helena—who knows nothing of the situation—tries to strike up a small affair with him, surrounding events also become strained. The slow rhythm of a provincial afternoon gives way to an oppressive and tense atmosphere. The hotel pool, at one point synonymous with pleasure, slowly becomes hell, a setting for all of Amalia's unsettling looks as she observes Dr. Jano, whom she ends up tormenting. The hotel also takes on a Dantesque dimension as Martel presents us with the personnel and patrons, who seem to be living in a permanent trap of emotional promiscuity and bottled up in unending discussions.

In that interview with the director, asking about her capacity to capture the conversational style common to provincial life, I found an all-encompassing answer that connected to this idea of total narration. The director explained that she thinks the most modern narrative structures exist in spoken language, and that she found her way into film precisely because oral traditions, bedtime stories, her grandmother's tales, and women chatting captivated her. She believes that those worlds of conversation hold the narrative structures that interest her most: the drifting, the ambiguous, and the hidden.

The Holy Girl helped to confirm Martel's success following her notable first feature film *La Ciénaga* (2001), as was also the case with a number of other key works of New Argentinean Film that came out around the same time, such as Lisandro Alonso's *Los Muertos* (2004) and *El Bonaerense* (2002) by Pablo Trapero, both second feature films for their authors. In the first few years of the 21st century, Argentinean cinema rose up with a radiant energy—and a sensitivity to match—that placed it amongst the world's film elite. As happens with these sorts of phenomenon, despite the differing styles of its most important members, all of the representatives were able to tell stories by looking at their surroundings, pulling directly from worlds they know, and combining their observational abilities with their filmmaking skills. Indeed, Martel demonstrated her own universe could reach more complex levels with her subsequent film, *The Headless Woman*, a film that covers various territories, sketching out ideas about guilt, biology, class and privilege, criminology, and people's convictions when facing moral dilemmas. A movie that, like a large part of her cinema, always leaves us with the feeling of being trapped in a space where evidence and uncertainty, what can and can't be, are constantly in conflict.

—Jerónimo Rodríguez

#10

Pan's Labyrinth

(Mexico, 2006)

He's politically savvy but also strongly in touch with his inner child. No matter that Mexican filmmaker Guillermo del Toro's *Pan's Labyrinth* deals with cerebral issues, such as the fissures in Spanish society following the Civil War and their human toll; his heart is in such non-human creations as the oversized magical cricket, the miniature friendly fairies, the anthropomorphic mandrake root, and the huge bilious toad.

His affection is strongest, though, for the two creatures played by del Toro stalwart Doug Jones: the tall, tipsy faun that doles out commands to the young female protagonist (the director told Jones to play him like a glam rocker, "more Jagger than Bowie"); and the quietly lethal Pale Man, a ghostly figure whose eyes are in the palms of his hands ("like stigmata," del Toro, a self-described "lapsed Catholic," told the *Observer*). They are constructs of animatronics and makeup more than CGI. In the same article, he explained that having previously directed the big-budget comic-book adaptations *Blade II* (USA, 2002) and *Hellboy* (USA, 2004) enabled him to make *Pan's Labyrinth* for a mere $11 million: "I love to play with the big toys—and to learn from them."

Del Toro is a compulsive sketcher whose pen-and-ink drawings of wacky and grotesque characters, on the pages of the leather-bound notebook he invariably carries with him, are never abstract; rather, they are rooted in some reality, albeit a surrealistic one, but a reality nonetheless.

In his first two features, *Cronos* (Mexico, 1993) and *Mimic* (USA, 1997), he blended the otherworldly with people and places very much of this world. With *The Devil's Backbone* (Mexico/Spain, 2001), set in Spain in 1939 at the tail end of the Civil War, he mixed in to the brew a potent political dimension. He returned to the tripartite formula in *Pan's Labyrinth*, which takes place in 1944, five years after the Fascists defeated the Republicans.

More than any film in recent memory, a plot synopsis does little justice to the film. Ten-year-old Ofelia (Ivana Baquero), volumes of fairy tales in hand, arrives after a long journey with her widowed, pregnant, and exhausted mother (Ariadna Gil) at the house of Mom's new husband, Captain Vidal (a nearly unrecognizable Sergi Lopez). A dedicated Franquist, the Captain also uses his home, a converted mill, as a military base from which his men are attempting to eradicate remnants of the Republican resistance who hide in the surrounding forest.

El laberinto del fauno / Pan's Labyrinth (2006)
Images courtesy of Telecinco Cinema

El laberinto del fauno / Pan's Labyrinth (2006)
Images courtesy of Telecinco Cinema

Obsessed with producing a male heir, Vidal cares little for his new bride and even less for his stepdaughter. Head servant Mercedes (Maribel Verdú, in a career-best performance) is the only member of the household to connect with the girl (humming her a lullaby that structures Javier Naverrete's brilliant soundtrack); she also clandestinely aids the resistance, which counts among its members her beloved brother, and among its sympathizers the doctor who attends the ill wife.

In the house, Ofelia meets some magical creatures but as the horrors around her mount, she escapes into a large nearby labyrinth, where she encounters many more. The faun instructs her to complete three tasks in order to regain her position as Princess Moanna of the Underworld. After her mother dies in childbirth, Ofelia kidnaps her newborn stepbrother, in response to the final command of the faun, who is in actuality testing her: Will she sacrifice the blood of an innocent to save herself?

Of the principal characters, only Mercedes survives, but Ofelia, in her final moments, visualizes not the darkness of death but instead a bright, Oz-like kingdom where she has a privileged place, and where her deceased mother and real father (Federico Luppi) occupy the thrones. Just before her brother shoots the Captain, Mercedes, who is holding his baby son, tells him that the boy will never know his father's name. The rupture with Fascism is clear.

In both *The Devil's Backbone* and *Pan's Labyrinth*, del Toro reserves the magical realm for leftists; he relegates Fascists to the earthly sphere. By masterfully depicting the supernatural (he originally studied special effects and makeup) as well as developing accessible narrative and formal strategies to convey his ideological position, he has built a distinctive niche for himself, one in which the boundaries between realism and imagination are blurred while the line between progressives and reactionaries is cut and dry.

Which is to say that he embraces the underlying concept of classical melodrama, the unambiguous opposition of good and evil—also the fundamental underpinning of the archetypal fairy tale, which, unless sanitized by the Disneys of this world and others who refuse to acknowledge the diversity of the human condition, takes place on the frontlines between the forces of light and the soldiers of darkness. Del Toro creates films for adults as well as children. He is, consciously or not, a disciple of the Brothers Grimm as well as of the heady writer Terri Windling, who notes in her introduction to the collection of essays, *Snow White, Blood Red*, the dangers posed when the near-perfect balance of the fairy tale is tampered with.

The dark path of the fairy tale forest lies in the shadows of our imagination, the depths of our unconscious. To travel to the wood, to face its dangers, is to emerge transformed by this experience. Particularly for children ... this ability to travel inward, to face fear and transform it, is a skill they will use all their lives. We do children—and ourselves—a grave disservice by censoring the old tales, glossing over the darker passages.

The popular film that best reflects a bastardization of that tradition is, of course, *The Wizard of Oz*, which del Toro references frequently in *Pan's Labyrinth*. (Ironically, *The Wizard of Oz* was released in 1939.) Victor Fleming's marvel did not venture onto political turf, but it did create an oneiric Technicolor universe inhabited by characters drawn from young Dorothy's banal black-and-white life on Auntie Em's no-nonsense Kansas farm, not to mention a host of inventive creatures. Yes, Ofelia dons ruby-red slippers when she finally gets to the oddly named Underworld, but at the tail end of her adventure she encounters not a fraudulent wizard but her idealized parents.

Del Toro goes even further. With a tilt or a pan, he seamlessly shuttles between the earthly and supernatural realms, lending them equal weight and validity. Unlike Dorothy post-Oz, Ofelia does not consider her journey an illusion. Even after her stepfather kills her, that world remains. A voiceover informs us that she, once again incarnated as the princess, reigned "with justice and a kind heart for many centuries." Just as the kingdom endures, so does the victory, for a short time anyway, of the small, outnumbered band of partisans on terra firma.

Del Toro adheres to an essential precept of both melodrama and the fairy tale: the highly determined symbol. The significance of each is overstated, so that the narrative flows unimpeded by unnecessary elaboration. The Captain is immutable; his inhumanity and vanity are apparent from the beginning. He is an arrogant authoritarian for whom discipline and obedience are the chief virtues.

In some other genres he might be considered a stereotype, some of the objects associated with him, clichés. Here they reveal aspects of his character. The cracked stopwatch he secretly possesses shows the time his military father died in battle; that is all the spectator needs to know to understand his macho rigidity. The key to the storehouse filled with ammunition and supplies that the captain gives to Mercedes recurs with regularity, and one just like it shows up in the blobby innards of the toad.

The labyrinth of the title, a word long associated with the Spanish Civil War, is not a maze; rather, it symbolizes a passage, one with several layers of meaning. There is the passage between the supernatural and the earthly, the one between childhood and adulthood, and, perhaps most significantly, the gateway between decades of dictatorship and the post-Franco era in which liberated Spaniards have made up for lost time. The latter period is the structural absence that del Toro flamboyantly celebrates.

—Howard Feinstein

Film Credits

LA CIÉNAGA

(Argentina/France/Spain, 103 min., 2001) Written and Directed by Lucrecia Martel. Producers: Ana Aizenberg, Diego Guebel, José María Morales, Mario Pergolini and Lita Stantic; Editor: Santiago Ricci; Director of Photography: Hugo Colace; Sound: Hervé Guyader, Emmanuel Croset, Guido Berenblum and Adrián De Michele. Cast: Mercedes Morán, Graciela Borges, Martín Adjemián and Leonora Balcarce.

AMORES PERROS

(Mexico, 154 min., 2000) Directed by Alejandro González Iñárritu; Written by Guillermo Arriaga. Producers: Guillermo Arriaga Jordán, Raúl Olvera Ferrer, Francisco González Compeán, Alejandro González Iñárritu, Pelayo Gutiérrez, Monica Lozano and Martha Sosa Elizondo; Editors: Luis Carballar, Alejandro González Iñárritu and Fernando Pérez Unda; Director of Photography: Rodrigo Prieto; Original Music: Gustavo Santaolalla; Sound: Martín Hernández. Cast: Emilio Echevarría, Gael García Bernal, Goya Toledo, Álvaro Guerrero and Vanessa Bauche.

LUZ SILENCIOSA / SILENT LIGHT / STELLET LICHT

(Mexico/France/Netherlands/Germany, 145 min., 2007) Written and Directed by Carlos Reygadas. Producers: Jeroen Beker, Jean Labadie, Carlos Reygadas, Jaime Romandía and Frans van Gestel; Editor: Natalia López; Director of Photography: Alexis Zabe; Sound: Sergio Díaz and Martín Hernández. Cast: Cornelio Wall, Maria Pankratz, Miriam Toews, Peter Wall, Jacobo Klassen and Elizabeth Fehr.

CIDADE DE DEUS / CITY OF GOD

(Brazil/France, 130 min., 2002) Directed by Fernando Meirelles and co-directed by Kátia Lund; Screenplay by Bráulio Mantovani, based on the novel by Paulo Lins. Producers: Andréa Barata Ribeiro, Marc Beauchamps, Daniel Filho, Hank Levine, Vincent Maraval, Mauricio Andrade Ramos, Donald K. Ranvaud, Juliette Renaud and Walter Salles; Editor: Daniel Rezende; Director of Photography: César Charlone; Sound: Martín Hernández. Cast: Alexandre Rodrigues, Leandro Firmino da Hora, Jonathan Haagensen, Douglas Silva, Alice Braga and Seu Jorge.

ÔNIBUS 174 / BUS 174

(Brazil, 150 min., 2002) Directed by José Padilha, co-directed by Felipe Lacerda; Written by José Padilha. Producers: José Padilha, Rodrigo Pimentel, and Marcos Prado; Editor: Felipe Lacerda; Director of Photography: Marcelo "Guru" Duarte and Ceza Moraes; Original Music: Sacha Amback, João Nabuco; Sound: Denilson Campos.

Y TU MAMÁ TAMBIÉN

(Mexico, 105 min., 2001) Directed by Alfonso Cuarón; Written by Alfonso Cuarón and Carlos Cuarón. Producers: Sergio Agüero, Alfonso Cuarón, Amy Kaufman, David Linde and Jorge Vergara; Editor: Alfonso Cuarón and Alex Rodríguez; Director of Photography: Emmanuel Lubezki; Sound: Ruy García. Cast: Diego Luna, Gael García Bernal and Maribel Verdú.

WHISKY

(Uruguay/Argentina/Germany/Spain, 99 min., 2004) Directed by Juan Pablo Rebella and Pablo Stoll; Written by Gonzalo Delgado, Juan Pablo Rebella and Pablo Stoll. Producers: Natacha Cervi, Fernando Epstein, Christoph Friedel and Hernán Musaluppi; Editor: Fernando Epstein; Director of Photography: Bárbara Álvarez; Original Music: Pequeña Orquesta Reincidentes; Sound: Catriel Vildosola y Daniel Yafalián. Cast: Andrés Pazos, Mirella Pascual and Jorge Bolani.

LA MUJER SIN CABEZA / THE HEADLESS WOMAN

(Argentina/Spain/France/Italy, 87 min., 2008) Written and Directed by Lucrecia Martel. Producers: Agustín Almodóvar, Pedro Almodóvar, Tilde Corsi, Verónica Cura, Esther García, Lucrecia Martel, Cesare Petrillo, Enrique Piñeyro, Vieri Razzini, and Marianne Slot; Editor: Miguel Schverdfinger; Director of Photography: Bárbara Álvarez; Sound: Guido Berenblum, Paula Dalgalarando and Martín Mainoli. Cast: María Onetto, Claudia Cantero, César Bordón, Daniel Genoud, Guillermo Arengo and Inés Efron.

LA NIÑA SANTA / THE HOLY GIRL

(Argentina/Spain/Italy/Netherlands, 106 min., 2004) Directed by Lucrecia Martel; Written by Lucrecia Martel with contributing writer Juan Pablo Domenech. Producers: Agustín Almodóvar, Pedro Almodóvar, Tilde Corsi, Esther García, Alfredo Ghirardo, Nora Kohen, Cesare Petrillo, Vieri Razzini, Gianni Romoli, Lita Stantic and Álvaro Urtizberea; Editor: Santiago Ricci; Director of Photography: Félix Monte; Original Music: Andrés Gerszenson; Sound: Guido Berenblum. Cast: Mercedes Morán, Carlos Belloso, Alejandro Urdapilleta, María Alche, Julieta Zylberberg and Mía Maestro.

EL LABERINTO DEL FAUNO / PAN'S LABYRINTH

(Mexico/Spain/USA, 120 min., 2006) Written and Directed by Guillermo del Toro. Producers: Belén Atienza, Álvaro Agustín, Alfonso Cuarón, David Ebner, Edmundo Gil, Elena Manrique, Bertha Navarro, Guillermo del Toro and Frida Torresblanco; Editor: Bernat Vilaplana; Director of Photography: Guillermo Navarro; Original Music: Javier Navarrete; Sound: Martín Hernández. Cast: Ivana Baquero, Sergi López, Maribel Verdú, Doug Jones and Ariadna Gil.

Survey Participants

Inés Aslán—Communications Officer, El Museo del Barrio

Graciela Berger Wegsman—Playwright / Journalist, *New York Daily News, Hora Hispana*

Rodrigo Brandão—Director of Publicity, Kino International

Roberto Busó-García—Founder, Alquimia Films

Fabiano Canosa—Film programmer

Jerry W. Carlson—Film professor, The City College & Graduate Center CUNY

Rebeca Conget—VP Acquisitions and Distribution, Film Movement

Gerard Dapena—Scholar of Hispanic cinemas and visual culture

Christian Del Moral—Film blogger, CineLatinoNY

Mario Díaz—Filmmaker / Film blogger

Howard Feinstein—Film critic, Screen / Programmer, Panorama and Sarajevo Film Festival

Cristina Garza—International Sales and Distribution, FiGa Films

Marcela Goglio—Programmer, Latinbeat (Film Society of Lincoln Center)

Pablo Goldbarg—Filmmaker / Writer, *Remezcla,* Cinema Tropical

Javier Guerrero—Director, 100% Venezuela (NYU Venezuelan Film Festival)

Carlos A. Gutiérrez—Co-Founding Director, Cinema Tropical

Paula Heredia—Filmmaker/editor, Casa Clementina

Jytte Jensen—Curator, MoMA Department of Film

Peter Lucas—Professor, Department of Photography and Imaging and Open Arts at the Tisch School of Arts at New York University

Yehudit Mam—Filmmaker / Blogger, The Grande Enchilada

Mary Jane Marcasiano—Special Events Advisor, Cinema Tropical / Programmer

Alberto Medina—Author / Associate professor, Columbia University

Micki Mihich—Filmmaker, film critic and blogger, *Dynamite Magazine* and *Dynamite Online*

Lucila Moctezuma—Film programmer

Nuria Net—Editor-in-Chief, Co-Founder, *Remezcla*

Louis Perego Moreno—Executive Producer, Skyline Features; President, NALIP-NY

Carmen Oquendo—Researcher and film curator, NYU

Jack Rico—Editor-in-Chief, ShowBizCafe.com

Alex Rivera—Filmmaker/founder SubCine

Jerónimo Rodríguez—Film critic/Host, *Toma 1* (NY1 Noticias)

Paul Julian Smith—Author, *The Cinema of Pedro Almodóvar and Amores Perros*

Roselly Torres—Distribution & Marketing Director, Third World Newsreel

Diana Vargas—Programmer, Havana Film Festival (NY) and Corto Circuito

Mónika Wagenberg—Co-Founding Director, Cinema Tropical

Naief Yehya—Film critic, *La Jornada, Milenio* / Author, *The Transformed Body, War and Propaganda*

Contributors

Gerard Dapena is a scholar of Hispanic Cinemas and Visual Culture. He has published and lectured on different aspects of Spanish and Latin American film and art history and taught at a number of colleges in the U.S.

Tamara L. Falicov is Associate Professor and Chair of the Department of Film and Media Studies at the University of Kansas. She is a core faculty member in the Center of Latin American Studies. Professor Falicov's specialty is the study of Latin American film industries, with particular focus on the cinemas of Argentina, the Southern Cone, and Cuba. She is the author of *The Cinematic Tango: Contemporary Argentine Film* (London: Wallflower Press, 2007).

Howard Feinstein is a film critic for Screen, Filmmaker, and other publications. He has been programming for the Sarajevo Film Festival since 1999, and lives in New York.

Misha MacLaird is a film writer and curator from Oakland, California. Her research on Mexico's post-1994 film industry was supported by a Fulbright-Hays award. She has recently published a book chapter on 1970s Mexican shark films and an interview on Amazonian werewolves.

David Oubiña earned his doctorate in the Arts and Humanities. He is a researcher for CONICET (the Argentine National Council of Scientific and Technical Research) and a professor at the Universidad del Cine and New York University in Buenos Aires. He is a member of the editorial board of *Cahiers du cinema: España* and Board of Directors of *Las ranas: Arte, ensayo, traducción*. He has written several books including: *Estudio sobre La ciénaga, de Lucrecia Martel* (Picnic, 2007), *Una juguetería filosófica. Cine cronofotografía y arte digital* (Manantial, 2009) and the forthcoming *El silencio y sus bordes. Modos de lo extremo en cine y literatura* (Fondo de cultura económica).

Jerónimo Rodríguez was born in Santiago, Chile. He is the critic-host for the film review television program, Toma Uno, on NY1 Noticias in New York City. He also has worked as a film columnist for and contributed articles to publications such as *Sports Illustrated Latino, People (en Español), Capital Magazine,* and *El Nuevo Canon*. Additionally, he served as script advisor on the feature film *Huacho*, which was selected for Cannes Critics' Week and the Toronto International Film Festival, and won the Sundance/NHK International Filmmakers Award. Jerónimo moved to the U.S. after graduating from law school.

Josefina Sartora is a Literature professor from Argentina, focusing her studies on myths, symbols and archetypes in the image, and on documentary film. She also studies the connection between art and philosophy. Her works about these subjects have appeared in several publications in Argentina and France. Her latest book—about Argentine documentaries and co-edited with Silvina Rival—is *Imágenes de lo real.* She contributes to *Le Monde Diplomatique* (Argentine edition) on cinema and cultural studies, and is a regular critic at www.otroscines.com and *Agenda del Sur.*

Paul Julian Smith is Distinguished Professor in the Hispanic and Luso-Brazilian Program at the Graduate Center, City University of New York. He is the author of fifteen books including: *Amores Perros* (BFI 2003), *Desire Unlimited: The Cinema of Pedro Almodóvar* (Verso, 2001) and *Spanish Screen Fiction: Between Cinema and Television* (Liverpool UP, 2009). He is a regular contributor to *Sight & Sound* and *Film Quarterly.*

Else R. P. Vieira has written and taught on a broad range of subjects including the politicization of the expression of the dispossessed and issues of gender and sexuality. Here last published book was *City of God in Several Voices: Brazilian Social Cinema as Action* (2005) and she is currently working on a project entitled *Screening Exclusion: Brazilian and Argentine Documentary Film-Making,* which compares the 21st century boom of the documentary in these two nations.

Naief Yehya is an industrial engineer, journalist, writer and cultural critic. His work deals mainly with the impact of technology, mass media, propaganda and pornography in culture and society. His most recent book is *Technoculture* (Tusquets, 2008).

Acknowledgments

It's been a remarkable journey since Monika Wagenberg and I were both students in the Cinema Studies Master's program at New York University, and were inspired by professor Bob Stam and his Brazilian cinema class to create a platform for the promotion of Latin American in New York City. From its very inception, Cinema Tropical—like filmmaking itself—has been a collaborative endeavor, which makes it practically impossible to thank all the people who have generously supported the organization and its mission throughout these years, including filmmakers, collaborators, colleagues, sponsors, interns, volunteers, and the audience itself.

I want to acknowledge the people that have been instrumental in the launching of the Cinema Tropical Awards and this ambitious initiative celebrating a decade of great Latin American cinema: Mary Jane Marcasiano, Ricardo Trejo, Primavera Salvá, Mara Behrens, Mario Díaz, Laura Martínez Ruiz-Velasco, Andrew Vargas-Stehney, Jacquie Baertschi, Julia Knobloch, Mark Robertson, and Ryan McManus. And of course, Bob Stam, Debbie Zimmerman, Margarita de la Vega Hurtado and Josh Siegel, members of our board of directors, who have also played an important role in the consolidation of the organization.

For this book in particular, I want to thank the enthusiasm and dedication of Jorge Pinto, who kindly offered this valuable platform to Latin American cinema. Additional thanks to Richard Shpuntoff, who was so gracious and committed in helping me edit this book, and to all of the contributing writers that accepted to participated in this dialogue. Last, but not least, I want to acknowledge the continued encouragement of my parents, Carlos M. Gutiérrez and Susana Casas.

To all of them I wish to express my most sincere and heartfelt gratitude.

Cinema Tropical Presents
The Ten Best Latin American Films of the Decade.

Presenting Partners:

Latino Heritage Network of
The New York Times Company

Sponsored by:

The Mexican Cultural
Institute of New York

CONSULATE GENERAL OF BRAZIL IN NEW YORK

Additional support by:

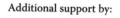

State of the Arts

NYSCA